Is It a Date or Just Coffee?

Is It a Date or Just Coffee?

The Gay Girl's Guide to Dating, Sex, and Romance

By Mo Brownsey

alyson books
los angeles | new york

MANUFACTURED IN THE UNITED STATES OF AMERICA.

THIS TRADE PAPERBACK ORIGINAL IS PUBLISHED BY ALYSON PUBLICATIONS,
P.O. BOX 4371, LOS ANGELES, CALIFORNIA 90078-4371.
DISTRIBUTION IN THE UNITED KINGDOM BY TURNAROUND PUBLISHER SERVICES LTD.,
UNIT 3, OLYMPIA TRADING ESTATE, COBURG ROAD, WOOD GREEN,
LONDON N22 6TZ ENGLAND.

FIRST EDITION: AUGUST 2002

07 08 09 **a** 10 9 8 7 6 5

ISBN 1-55583-727-1
ISBN-13 978-1-55583-727-3

LIBRARY OF CONGRESS CATALOGING-IN-PUBLICATION DATA
BROWNSEY, MO.
    IS IT A DATE OR JUST COFFEE? : THE GAY GIRL'S GUIDE TO DATING, SEX, AND
ROMANCE / BY MO BROWNSEY.—1ST ED.
    ISBN 1-55583-727-1   ISBN-13 978-1-55583-727-3
    1. LESBIANS—UNITED STATES—SOCIAL NETWORKS. 2. LESBIANS—UNITED
STATES—SEXUAL BEHAVIOR. 3.DATING (SOCIAL CUSTOMS)—UNITED STATES.
4. INTERPERSONAL RELATIONS—UNITED STATES. 5. FEMALE FRIENDSHIP—
UNITED STATES. I. TITLE.
HQ75.6.U5 B67 2002
306.76"63—DC21   2002025558

CREDITS
A VERSION OF SOME ESSAYS ORIGINALLY APPEARED ON MATCH.COM.
COVER DESIGN BY LOUIS MANDRAPILIAS.
COVER PHOTOGRAPH BY LYNNLY LABOVITZ.

Table of Contents

Introduction:
Is It a Date or Just Coffee?

Since the dawn of time, gay girls of all sorts—be they dykes, lesbians, bisexual, bi-curious, queer, or transgendered—have never been able to figure out whether or not they're on a date until, say, they're showering together or trying to find those pesky undergarments. Even Sappho (7th century BCE) had problems figuring out if it was just a sister-to-sister lute duet or a more amorous situation. Gay-girl dating is confusing, delirious, wonderful, and absurd. I mean, you did buy this book—or if you're browsing, I heavily suggest you buy it immediately, because we could all use a little help in this area and definitely a good laugh or 20.

Allow me to illustrate with a classic coffee-or-date situation: Let's say two single gay girls are introduced, hit it off, exchange numbers, then meet for the ubiquitous cup of coffee. Now, it could be that they're both avid snowboarders and that's their supposed reason for getting together. Still, at least one of them is probably thinking, *Is there a spark? Do we have chemistry? Am I delusional or did she just flirt with me?* Knowing whether you're on a date is particularly tricky for women, since we've all been heterosexually socialized and still have only vague notions of what constitutes pushy, aggressive, or unwanted attention in potential dating situations. If you're femme-identified, you may wait for your butch date to be the aggressor, but I know so many shy butches who agonize over that initial asking out that they're practically waiting for the femme to do everything but pin them to the wall. So even in the butch/femme world, this sticky situation often arises.

Why do gay girls encounter this so often? When a straight woman meets a straight guy at a party and they exchange numbers, it's unlikely that they'll get together and discuss the weather. ("Hey, what about that cold front over Montana?") More than likely, they'll both know they're on a first date and act accordingly. ("Hey, what about that cold front over Montana? You have the most beautiful eyes.") I realize I may be going out on a limb here—not being straight myself— but since 98% of characters on TV and in movies are straight, I've learned quite a bit about how nongay girls date. Straight people definitely enjoy a much higher frequency of knowing exactly when they are on a date.

In fact, many lesbians suffer from what I call Optional Dating Disorder (ODD). This is a rampant affliction whereby two women start out the evening thinking they're on a date, but by the end of the night at least one of them is thoroughly convinced that it isn't a date at all, never was, and why is this woman trying to kiss me good night? A lesbian in the throes of ODD won't even get the obvious hints. If you suffer from this, you know exactly what I mean. For example, let's say your ODD kicks in after the appetizers and before the main course. Therefore, when your dinner partner very seductively tries to feed you some sexy dessert, like chocolate-covered strawberries, you'll probably do something knee-jerk and reactionary like bite your date's finger, which isn't the best solution, since (a) she may enjoy being bitten and thus be further encouraged in her amorous exploits; (b) she might be an attorney who will sue your pants off in lieu of getting your pants off; or (c) you may hurt a perfectly nice woman's feelings to the point that she seeks professional help.

I realize that last part sounds very sad indeed. But in actuality, if your date is a bona fide gay girl, chances are she's already in therapy, has been, or is a therapist herself. Therefore, the ODD sufferer should feel like dirt for at least one day, but no more than three. Unfortunately, if this is you, you are not alone. Many, many lesbians suffer from this disorder.

On the other end of the lesbian-dating spectrum lies DDD (Delayed Dating Disorder). This occurs when a couple decides they're on a date when they start making room for each other's stuff on the bathroom shelf. This isn't as uncommon as the casual observer would think and is actually related to ODD. For many lesbians, the process of even fig- uring out whether they're on a date is so distressing that they'd rather get married *before* they date.

And lest it would appear that I am judging without expe- riencing, I know about ODD firsthand. I was once on a first get-together with a very attractive, famous comic whom everyone in San Francisco but myself knew to be partnered with an equally famous gay-girl photographer. At some point during dinner, she mentioned her famous partner in an "us" sort of way. My jaw dropped. We were both momentarily embarrassed. Then my ODD kicked in and I suddenly real- ized this wasn't a date at all. I hadn't really wanted it to be a date anyway, so what was there to be embarrassed about? She wasn't even my type. The fact that I don't apparently have a type flies right out of my mind.

This was more than 10 years ago. Since then, I've learned my lesson. Now I simply ask, "Is this a date?" Or if I'm doing the asking, I say, "I'd like to take you out to dinner on a *date.*" Novel concept, huh? This way, if I'm going to be rejected, I don't have to waste any time on the pretense of a friendship— or blow my paycheck on a lobster dinner only to realize she's just looking for a steady ride to take her snowboarding.

So, welcome to the *Mo World* of gay-girl dating, sex, romance, and more! For your convenience, this book is handily divided into tidy little sections. You say you to need to skip straight to the relationships section? Because yours is starting to have a *Titanic* feel to it, without the kind of "going down" you had in mind? Go right to it. Had yet *another* Internet date that belongs in *Ripley's Believe It or Not?* Zip right to my unique retelling of Internet dates gone by the wayside. Still intensely feeling that breakup hangover? I'm all over it. Trying to figure out how to end your relationship before the next centennial celebration? I've got you covered. Lest you think it's all downside, there's a whole section on romance in this book, but let's face it, that's the easy stuff. When you're that delirious, who needs to laugh away the pain? In fact, if you were madly in love, you probably wouldn't have even picked up this book, unless it's for a friend in need.

Why did I write this book? Because they gave me money? Because I've had more bizarre dates/romances in gay-girl herstory than anyone I know? Because I'm crazy about all gay girls and everything that goes with them? (If you answered yes to any or all of the above, you'd be right.) In fairness, I'm an artist and have more time to think about these things than most people. See, I can get into all these great, not-so-great, and downright horrifying situations, then write about them. Nifty, huh? Though I suspect I'm not alone here; even those with full-time mega-careers have probably had their share of gay-girl love: the epic, the mundane, and everything in-between. It is therefore my contention that pretty much any gay girl can find herself in one of these torpid states (except New Jersey, if you can help it—though I hear Hoboken is pretty cool these days).

part one

Single Too?

- how to tell if you are in fact single
- how to get back to normal hygiene habits
- helpful tips on remaking your home for one
- and other life- or at least psyche-saving ideas

How to Tell if You're Single

At first glance this may seem simple, but for the gay girl this may not always be the case. There are, of course, telltale signs: Half the CDs are gone, you eat red licorice for dinner while watching reruns of *Bay Watch,* and you're back in therapy (if you ever left, that is). But many a gay girl has become single without her full, conscious knowledge.

Unconscious singlehood can manifest itself in several ways. Most commonly, a couple will have a big fight followed by a compromise that they'll try an open relationship—for now, anyway. The one to suggest this is generally the one who finds another lover first (if she hasn't already). If you're not the one to propose an open relationship, you may already be borderline single without knowing it.

What are the subtle signs? For starters, your girlfriend of X years will walk around the house for weeks humming and generally appearing too damn happy. Your sex life has not quite kicked in yet since your fight, but you're getting along so much better, really, you tell yourself—like a mantra: "It's better, it's better, it's better." What you don't know, however, is that your lover has already snagged another lover, whether she has crossed "that line" or not. In fact, it could be that your girlfriend does have a sex life; it just doesn't include you.

If you suspect she does have a "girl on the side," here are a few things you might consider: Ask her point-blank (be strong—remember that truth does not necessarily equal beauty, virtue, or happy news) or establish a clause up front that if you plan to act on the open R (relationship), you'll tell each other. This will not only save you a lot of anxiety, but if she omits the information, for sure you'll get first dibs on the apartment/house. (For gay girls in San Francisco or New York City, this is of particular significance.)

I was once in an open phase of a relationship that was going downhill. My girlfriend and I instituted the "you have to tell the other person if it goes it goes beyond one date" clause. Though the agreement was mutual, I'd been the one to suggest it. At the time, I had no sexual prospects even vaguely on the horizon, especially since I never have a wandering eye once I'm "with" someone. (OK, I did once—no, twice, but the latter still lived with her sort-of ex-girlfriend, and I didn't think we were exactly committed. But I swear that's it.)

Within a week, in a sequence of events usually reserved for a "yeah, right, that'll happen" scene in a Hollywood movie, I met someone I had major electric chemistry with even before we kissed. As my primary R was LD (long distance) I actually flew down to tell my girlfriend face-to-face that there was to be a second date.

At this point she asked, "Do you think it'll go beyond that?" I said yes. I knew I wasn't in love with this woman and probably never would be, but I couldn't fight this tidal-wave chemistry. My girlfriend promptly broke up with me. I tried to explain to her that it was all pheromones, but that actually hurt her more.

So a word of caution: Never tell your open-R lover that you have incredible hots for another woman. It's in very bad form.

I thought that emphasizing how much I loved her and how important our relationship was would override any feelings of insecurity she might have had. No. No, no, no, no.

Another way you may not realize you are in fact single: She's moved out, but you both believe this will improve the R. You still talk every day, the tears have dried, you cuddle and sleep together…well, once a week or so. She seems to have her answering machine on a lot—does that mean something? You are single. Proceed accordingly. At the very least, start scanning the personals. And always, always, always, remember that you're a babe. You were and you will be again.

Wash That Ex Right Out of Your Hair

It's over. You're done crying over the photos, the half-burned candles, and all that extra room on the bathroom shelves. It's now time to weed out the visual remains of your relationship. Especially if you cohabited, which for any lesbian relationship over, say, two years—for some, two months—there's a 98% chance of this being the case.

Your ability to rid your home of the physical reminders, of course, may be partially dependent upon your disposable income. If you inherited the "bought-together" bed, sofa, or dresser, you may not be able to replace it immediately. I must admit that I once inherited my ex-girlfriend's dresser. At the time, I was still in grad school, so buying a new dresser was out of the question. But years later when I finally put that dresser out in front of my house with a FREE sign taped to it, to me it meant more than just "You can take this." It felt so liberating to finally have the last bit of that relationship completely gone. In fact, I marveled that I hadn't taken on a second job years before to rid myself of that dresser. What was I thinking?

What you can do immediately is change the entire floor plan of your living space, which I highly recommend. Caution: This may also move around a disc or two, so be careful—for those under 30, I'm not referring to a CD—but it'll be worth it. If home decor is not your strong suit, fetch one of your artier gay boyfriends to help you out. You'll laugh more, and he'll *fag-shui* your apartment into a stupor. I mean that in the most complimentary way. We are family, after all—as dysfunctional and oddly matched as we may be.

Most importantly, buy new sheets. If you can afford it, throw in a new duvet or bedspread. The old sheets will make you mad, sad, or potentially, at a weak moment, full of desire. Believe me, that new set of "just for me" sheets will cheer you up more than you'd think. It will be both symbolic and self-indulgent—and you need both.

Now to the obvious: All us/her photos must be removed (unless you've already burned them). I must admit, burning two or three of them does feel pretty damn good. If you're the spiritual type, throw in some sage and call it a cleansing ritual. Sometimes petty revenge is the elixir of life. As for the rest of the photos, put them in a box, stash them way back in the closet with your high school yearbooks, those vacuum cleaner bags you can never find, and all that other stuff you don't use/need but somehow can't part with.

At some point when you've had at least that first post-breakup "starter lover," you may be able to gaze at some of the photos with fondness, or just leave them in the back of the closet for the next year or 10. If you burned all of the photos, this is clearly a nonissue and you now have more room in the back of your closet.

If you and your girlfriend didn't live together, buy new sheets anyway. The fact that she has never slept on them should be worth the price of admission. And take her number off speed dial—immediately. OFF. OFF. OFF. This is not vindictive; this is healthy. Even if you're in the "want to stay friends" category, take her number off speed dial for at least a year.

After that first bout of crying and wandering aimlessly about your apartment and dialing all but her last number every hour on the hour, it's now time to take action. If you're one of those people who ceases to take care of her bodily needs after a breakup (eating, sleeping, showering, etc.), here are some ideas:

1. Take a shower—a full one—for at least 20 minutes. Rub off that nasty breakup crud that's layering your skin like mold on bread. If while shaving (if you do), you become too fascinated with the blade, jump out of the shower immediately and phone a therapist or a friend. I'm cheap and sincerely doubt that my blue Bic disposable razor could incur more than a Band-Aid's worth of harm, but you can't be too careful.

2. Unplug your phone and answering machine if you suffer from the "I know she's going to call and beg for my forgiveness any minute now" affliction. But just for a day or two. My reasoning: During one especially pitiful breakup I forced myself to unplug my phone for three days. I did this because I was so obsessed with her calling and begging for forgiveness that I had scripted several elaborate and well-worked scenes in my head. I knew my situation was bad when the dialogue leaked out of my head and I was actually speaking the scenes out loud. I played both parts. Her: contrite and emotional. Me: pained but stoic—all while wearing

the same three-day-old sweatpants and paint-stained rugby shirt. Barring institutionalization, I don't think it gets worse than this. (Though I'm not counting stalking, since that particular permutation of heartbreak has never appealed to me. I have several friends, though, who in their breakup agony casually drove past their ex's out-of-the-way house five or 50 times a day.)

During my wretched breakup period, I had even developed a time-saving technique to stay in denial about my slovenliness: I'd turn up the cuffs of the rugby shirt as they got stained. By day 3, they were past my elbows. The irony: I knew she would never call. The odds of any of my many scenarios ever happening were up there with Mr. Shrub (our "not really if you counted all the votes" prez) taking money out of the military budget to fund the Lesbian Avengers. So if you're constantly hoping she'll call (even though you know she won't), unplugging can help. By day 4, my friends descended upon my apartment like the angels they were— and threw me in the shower. (See Step 1.)

3. As you probably haven't eaten several of the major food groups in the last week (or 10), go out for a meal with a friend. During one particularly hard breakup, I subsisted solely on Ben and Jerry's Chunky Monkey, red licorice, coffee, and HBO. For months. I'm surprised I didn't get scurvy.

Be sure to pick the restaurant carefully. No froufrou nouvelle cuisine (an asparagus spear adorned by a nasturtium and one raspberry). Uh-uh. If a friend isn't available, go by yourself. Yes, that's right. You can do it. You may want to pick a more low-key place, say, a sweet café or diner-type place. And no ordering in. That would defeat the purpose of the whole exercise.

You'll be amazed at how the world is still there. Dry cleaners to the right, Copymat to the left. The bus kiosk glass has been shattered again. (That was for the city girls. For my rural gay girls: cows to the left, grain storage to the right...) All is as you left it before you took the breakup header.

4. Wear a favorite shirt that does *not* remind you of her. Wear the jeans you know make your butt look cute, or if there's been too much ice cream, a fetching pair of overalls and kicky shoes should do the trick. Wear colors you like. In San Francisco, Los Angeles, or New York City, that means black or...black.

Then, there's always retail therapy—but for some it's already an addiction, so I hesitate to recommend it. Compromise: Go to the Gap with a $100 limit. That way you won't end up looking like a not-quite-right Britney Spears— or for the butches, Ricky Martin (only butcher). OK, no one wants to look like Ricky Martin, except maybe in a retro drag king number. He's so 1999.

5. Depending on how long you've been in seclusion, you may need a refreshed hairdo. Warning: Do not get an impulsive, totally different haircut from what you had—at least not the first time out. You'll probably end up with something too trendy, too conservative, too...well, not *you*. This will only confirm your twisted notion that you are not cute enough to be loved. I know that I personally have agonized over a bad haircut to the level of psychosis. But that's just me. This

warning goes doubly for butches, whose coifs generally range from shaved scalp to one inch of hair. When less is more, it's important to get it right.

Now that you have the basics, it's time to rejoin the living. In person. Not by phone, E-mail, or psychic messages. Now, you may have begged off numerous social offerings for some time and feel awkward proposing an outing. Relax. You're thinking too much. Each and every one of your friends—gay, straight, bi, trans, and undecided—has gone through a heartbreak. Think of it this way: It will do them good to help out a buddy.

A word of caution here: Do not, I mean, do NOT under any circumstances go to any of the old haunts of your ex or your ex-couplehood. This will only remind you of good times that may or may not have existed. You may also have the unfortunate experience of seeing her gleefully enter with her new amour, whom your loyal friends will assure you you're way cuter than—even if she's Janet Jackson or Jodie Foster. Chances are, the new couple will be all smiles, generosity, and satiated sex—in glaring neon letters. This is simply something you need not subject yourself to. Why? To prove you don't care? That it doesn't hurt? You're dreaming. A few months from now, maybe.

If you should meet her on the outside, do your damnedest not to crumble and run. With any luck at all, if you wait her out, *she'll* do that. Now, that would be worth the outing. This is, of course, if you haven't gone the ubiquitous "let's stay friends" route.

Having completed this regime, you should now have that core self-respect that starts to bud once you realize that anyone with such great friends must be a pretty good person. Plus, your pals will have told you all their worst romance horror stories, embellishing them with delight. And hopefully you'll all get a good laugh on a full belly.

Keep repeating to yourself that heartbreak/romance accounts for 80% of all art and 98% of all country music. There must be a reason for that, and there is: It's heaven when it's good and it sucks big time when it's gone. Avoiding Heartbreak Hotel could be a full-time job for some of us. But believe me, once you're on that road, no matter how many pit stops and detours you manage to take, you will end up at the same place. It is definitely *The Road Most Traveled*. The less you resist, the quicker you'll get it over with. I know, I know, it hurts. And delaying pain is so damn tempting, but actually it creates a whole new kind of pain, so really you're not doing yourself any favors. That said, it's over when it's over, and timing is everything. Unfortunately, there's never a good time for a heartbreak. This is where I should throw in how it is "better to have loved and lost than never to have loved at all." (Though lofty philosophical sayings can be so damn annoying when all you want is revenge, relief, take-out pizza on demand, and an incredibly comfortable couch.)

Vacations, Single Style

It's time to get out of town, away from the familiar (after all, it does breed contempt), and generally get a new take on life. Will it be all-night dancing in Key West or a crack-of-dawn hike to the top of a trail/mountain/volcano? Do you want to learn to snorkel? Or maybe you just want to lie on the beach with a trashy detective novel and an iced tea, regular or Long Island. And being single, you do have the advantage of not having to endure that de rigueur pre-trip fight with your lover.

So many decisions and one suggestion: Bring a friend. Solitude is great for three or four days, but after that you'll find yourself chatting at length with the checkout clerk, concierge, forest ranger, or Porta Potti guy—and it won't be pretty. We are expressive beings by nature, and taking pictures and writing lengthy journal entries only goes so far. For most of us, that is. Sure, there are those stoic loner types, who in my secret heart I envy for their ability to store knowledge and emotion like stacks in the library. They rarely volunteer a word unless directly asked. Assuming you are not one of those noble creatures, I repeat: Bring a friend.

Where to now? If you're both gay, or your straight friend is up for something new, you'll probably want to go someplace that might offer the alluring possibility of a fleeting romance (or a few nights of fun).

Provincetown, Massachusetts, in the summer is *très* gay

and lots of fun, but hotels are usually booked ages ahead of time. So that's one destination you must plan ahead for. (I'm convinced that's one of the ways people couple off: One person is the slightly anal plan-ahead type, while the other wings it.) So if you're not a planner and still want to try out P-Town, check the various campgrounds on the Cape—that lezzie camping gene will kick in if need be. If you are so *not* into camping, P-Town's neighbor, Truro, despite its name, can be quite lovely and perhaps not so booked up. Oh, and there's always Key West and of course Fire Island for you sun-and-sand types.

I just happen to know more about P-Town, being one of the zillions of stand-up comics littering Commercial Street. Entertainers have to pigeonhole people on the beach and the main drag. By that I mean the comics actually ask people as they walk by to come to their show: "Here's a handy quarter-page flyer with all the information. Really—I'm funny." Comedy: It's nothing but glamour.

Grab one of those gay guides and see what's happening in the general vicinity of where you'd like to go. Plenty of places may surprise you. Believe it or not, Salt Lake City has a thriving queer nightlife and is surrounded by all kinds of natural wonders. You can hike by day and relax with the wholesome-looking Mormon of your choice by night. But be warned: If the guide says "local bar," they're not kidding. Unless your idea of a good time involves rescuing aging alcoholics, stay away. A local queer bookstore or Metropolitan Community Church offers more and better opportunities of the dating variety. And definitely a much better atmosphere.

To be absolutely sure you'll be in good company, you may want to try Olivia Cruises, an all-girl weekend event, or one of the many women's music festivals—if that's your style. In fact, I've worked as a comic on five Olivia vacations: Alaska, Montreal, a Caribbean cruise, and the Playa Blanca, Mexico, Club Med (twice).

The best cruise was the one to Alaska. It was 1992, and no one had ever heard of an all-lesbian cruise. *Ever.* This was pre-lesbian chic—pre-lipstick or even pre-Chapstick lesbian culture. So there we were, 900 women on a boat going into these teeny-tiny port towns where there are 20 men to each woman. These local guys hear that 900 women on a boat are coming to town. And then...*we* get off. You could feel their crushing disappointment. All those women and no one to flirt with. These guys knew what many women (gay and straight) have felt for years: *I shaved for this?* The days of lurking shame-filled lesbianism were over. At least in Juneau, Alaska, on June 23, 1992.

Incidentally, this was the same cruise that the scarily brilliant comic Margaret Cho refers to in her solo show/film, *I'm the That One I Want.* The comic lineup on that particular cruise was truly stellar: Marga Gomez, Karen Williams, Miss Cho, and...me? I do believe that was *my* 15 minutes of fame.

At one point during the cruise, I looked around and realized why I felt so happy: It was like one big slumber party. Food and games and screaming girls everywhere you looked. All-night discos, casinos, piano lounges, magnificent views. OK, so my basement stateroom didn't have a view, but I only crept back there to change clothes and collapse into a heap after staying up all night to watch the sun *not* go down. And it was so *safe*. It was like being in this utopian "Herland." I hadn't realized how, at a white-noise level, unsafe I'd felt in my day-to-day life.

After five of these trips, I did notice that the colder the cruise, the older the clientele; the warmer the destination, the younger the women. It probably has to do with the choice between wearing parkas or thong bathing suits. And Olivia always has a coordinated singles group so everyone can meet each other. This helps, since the entire lesbian nation is waiting for someone else to ask them to dance.

A story I can't resist telling is the one time the gay men's Atlantis group overlapped with the Olivia group at Club Med. The Olivia staff and entertainers got there a day early and got to witness Atlantis's last day. Can you say (or spell) "bacchanalian"? Those boys set an all-time Club Med record for number of drinks sold during the 3-5 P.M. tea dance. I was warned by comic Mark Davis not to go wandering on the beach that night—last chance for romance and all that. And he wasn't kidding.

For an entirely different though festive and lots-of-women-type vacation, there are women's events all over the country that require little money and less planning. One of the events I'm very familiar with is the Russian River Women's Weekend in Guerneville. I've been comedienne/mistress of ceremonies at one of the two large resort hotels there at least six times. Held the first weekend in May and the last weekend in September, this event is a long-standing tradition in Northern California. You can stay at one of the gay resorts or hotels or camp at several local spots.

Thousands or at least 1,000 women descend upon small, isolated Guerneville, whose sole claim to fame is the Russian River. There's almost nothing in the town except a strip of gay-themed stores—should you need anything, and I mean *anything* rainbow—three or four bars, and uniformly bad coffee. I bring my own and make it in my room. I'm convinced gay people go there because there are only two turns during the entire 90-minute drive from San Francisco.

The people who live up there are mostly rural and working-class and must be used to gay people of all stripes by now. Still, it must be odd to grow up in a town that during the week is very rural America but come Friday welcomes leather daddies. That's got to be disorienting—or at the very least educational.

To give you a more intimate portrait of this lesbian wonderland, here are a few excerpts from the diary I kept during one visit.

Friday, May 4, 2001

Town's packed. Lesbians with that short-in-front/long-in-back hairdo from 1982 dot the land. It's not necessarily their fault; that's just the style they adopted moments after kissing their first woman, and they never got over it. Sort of like my uncle, now approaching 60, who still sports an Elvis coif. The age range is from gay girls just barely 21—"Please let me in the bar"—to the over-40 crowd. It's *loud.* Women whoop and holler in a general letting loose of the id. The smaller (hence more homophobic) the hometown, the louder the scream. Most single women are determined to meet *somebody* this weekend, and drinking and screaming appears to be the most direct method. I'm too tired to leave my hotel room, knowing that tomorrow I'll be telling jokes off and on for five hours. By the looks of things around here, I'll need all my strength.

Saturday, May 5, 2001

Women claim their lounge chairs by dawn. At 9 A.M. the entire poolside is littered with sweatshirts, towels, and, for the newly out, rainbow towels. I hit the stage at 12:30.

Most of these women have been trying to pace themselves so they won't pass out before the wet T-shirt contest, the day's finale set to start at 3:30. Being an ardent feminist and modest person by nature, you can only imagine how much I've looked forward to this event. I open the contest by commenting, "I know the lesbian nation has come a long way: We too can borrow games from frat boys. I want to make it clear, though, that because this is a gay-girl wet T-shirt contest, it's not about size. Large or tiny, all breasts are lovely!" I get a screaming round of applause for this and am reassured that feminism has not completely died. Oh, and every dollar raised goes to women's breast cancer research.

During the contest, someone pays $20 to throw me in the pool! At least I had time to take off my watch and $90 sneakers. Remember: glamour. I am admonished by one veteran "water babe" (the gal who fills the buckets from the pool) that I'm supposed to be commenting on the breasts. I smile blandly and uncomprehendingly, as though the music is too loud.

Sunday, May 6, 2001

The show starts very low-key. (The phrase "trying to raise the dead" comes to mind. But then the "Show Us Your Tattoo" contest gets the crowd's attention, and it's smooth sailing from here on out. I surprise myself by realizing I've developed an affection for these women and am having a fairly hilarious time of it—even after one drunk jock dyke picks me up as though I'm a bag of chips and starts heading for the pool. In my most intimidating voice I say, "Don't do this. I'm working!" but this doesn't stop her, so $90 sneakers and all, I get thrown in the pool and I am not happy. Glamour. It's all glamour.

Today's big event is the "Not Necessarily Ms. Right, But Ms. Right Now Commitment Ceremony." I enjoy coming up with the fake vows, such as:

"I do not want to know your horoscope."

"I do not want to know your cats' names."

"I promise to adore your body to the exclusion of all others for the next...six hours."

"If you get in a bad mood, I'm outta here."

"If you run out of money, I'm outta here."

"If your problematic ex-girlfriend shows up, I'm *really* outta here."

Women exchange nickel rings, people applaud, and I finally get off stage. And with so many women still sitting poolside, there *is* the possibility that my Ms. Right might be right under my nose. Because, after all, sisterhood is beautiful, but a new date is even better.

◆ ◆ ◆

These are but a few suggestions. So, single girl, plan yourself a sweet little vacation and mix and mingle with other eligible gay girls. Packing's a drag (no pun intended, ahem) and finding out how your shorts fit this year can set you back a day or two, but I say go to the nearest Gap and get yourself the basic baggy khaki shorts, a few new T-shirts, and call it a day.

Dream Lover: The List

I want my dream lover. Period. To this end, I've decided to improve the quality of my life, body, mind, and spirit; to achieve my potential, both creatively and spiritually. Oh, and to not use my credit cards at the end of the month—no matter how much I require Mexican takeout or those cute French zip-up ankle boots. To take a closer look at my choice of mates—not soul mates, but more like date mates—I came up with a couple of lists: what I do want and what I don't want in a lover. Interestingly, the "stuff I don't want" list was considerably easier to write than the "stuff I do want" list. Why is it always so easy to conjure up the bad, the painful, the ugly?

I will not date:

- any woman who has named herself after something in nature, including spices. Examples: Blizzard, Zoysia, Turmeric, Pigweed, Pepper, Hemlock.
- anyone who has a habit of starting every other sentence with the phrase, "Don't take this personally, but…"
- women who always wear really tall platform shoes, even to go to the bathroom—at home.
- women who call me Mo before I let them (OK, it's a control issue, but it's my list).
- women who bail on a first date without a doctor's or funeral director's note, (sporting a cast or neck brace the next time I see you will do, however).
- women who, after I tell them I work freelance in the

arts, ask me what I really want to be when I grow up. (Answer: more polite than you.)

• women who find almost anything else in the restaurant more interesting than me, including folding her napkin so excessively that I feel compelled to ask if she ever thought of taking up origami.

• any woman who doesn't identify as gay, lesbian, bisexual, or queer but just "dates women."

• a woman who refuses to see films with subtitles and claims that, "If I wanted to read a book, I'd have stayed home and finished that Nancy Drew."

I want to date:

• women who recognize and appreciate my sensitivity and unique qualities—intuitively, of course—so I can stay in denial of my more neurotic characteristics for yet another year.

• women of great strength—physically, emotionally, and mentally—so that they can not only carry a conversation, but also carry me to safety should I need it.

• women who make my heart flutter, not from a panic attack, but out of abject "Oh, God, I'm in heaven (and then some)" desire.

• women who make me laugh so hard it hurts. Laughing is next to godliness—cleanliness is good, but it won't keep you from murdering your boss, siblings, or landlords. Laughing is especially good with a lover.

Is she out there? I think so. I've met and fallen in love with her several times. She's always different than I thought, but then again, so am I.

Test Your Readiness-to-Date IQ

Pick the statement from each group that best describes your present attitude.

1. There's a deluxe all-girl dance party, and all your friends are going. You:

(a) Turn down the invitation and stay home to deep-clean your bathroom.

(b) Go dancing but don't notice anyone outside of your group of buddies.

(c) Attend the event and end up nasty-dancing with a stranger whose number you promptly lose.

2. A friend of a friend of a friend would like your phone number. You:

(a) Don't give it to her, since your pets have such unique personalities, who needs to leave home?

(b) Give her your number and spend the next 48 hours alternately hoping that she *will* or she *won't* call.

(c) Get her number, count the hours until the "neediness" time period is over, then end up calling early anyway.

3. Which statement most accurately describes you?

(a) You still have a picture of your ex-girlfriend in a drawer (facedown but within easy access).

(b) You find yourself in a store looking at all the great art cards and wonder to whom you could send this especially cool one. Then you realize you sent it to your ex over a year ago.

(c) You're so horny, you've bought an electric generator for your vibrator.

4. Which statement comes closest to summing up your present state?

(a) You haven't bought post-breakup new sheets yet because you've been too busy picking the lint off your sweater.

(b) You might accept the blind date your friends have cooked up for you—mostly to get them off your case.

(c) The guy at the video store has a very clear idea of how your sexual tastes run. The camouflage high-tone Emma Thompson flicks you rent are fooling no one.

5. You meet a woman you have immediate chemistry with. You:

(a) Literally flee the scene.

(b) Are sure to give and get last names—someone in the gay-girl grapevine will know who she is.

(c) Start eyeing the furniture possibilities or Rolodexing in your mind the closest private space…say, your place?

6. A woman asks you out. You:

(a) Stutter that you have plans, no matter what date

she suggests. And you do have plans: the bathroom,
the pets, the reruns of *Law and Order*…

(b) Are attracted to her, so you suggest "coffee" instead.

(c) Are very attracted, and your libido and pheromones
kick in so fast you're scared they're visible.

7. Melissa Etheridge, k.d. lang, and Ani DiFranco are in town for a once-in-a-lifetime concert, and everyone you know is going. You:

(a) Claim you've developed a sudden phobia of crowds.

(b) Definitely are going with your friends: There are sure
to be plenty of babe sightings.

(c) Got your ticket the day the concert went on sale and
have promised yourself that you aren't going to bed
that night without snagging at least one phone number
or a breakfast guest.

8. All you seem to think about these days is:

(a) Taking night classes and the next time you'll get
to deep-clean that bathroom.

(b) Whether you really want to go through that awkward
first-date kiss/no-kiss thing ever again.

(c) Hot, sweaty, mind-blowing 24-hour she-love sex
marathons—and this is while you're driving to work.

9. These days your social life most closely resembles:

(a) Hanging out at your friends/relatives with children
and spending at least one or both weekend nights
at their place.

(b) Making a point at least every couple weeks to go to a gay-girl/lesbian something, even if it's just the natural foods store.

(c) Systematically rotating going to all the queer-girl places in your town so you don't end up at that same café daily (unless you have a crush on the barista).

10. In your spare time, you:

(a) Get to the bottom of all that mail you never deal with and write actual snail-mail cards to several elderly relatives.

(b) Tentatively surf the personal ads on PlanetOut but never write to anyone.

(c) Obsessively check your PlanetOut personal ad E-mail and surf other I-dating sites daily.

Scoring:

A= 1 point   B= 3 points   C= 5 points

40-50

You are definitely ready to date. If you scored a perfect 50, you're so ready to date that it hurts. (I won't say where—you already know.)

20-39

You could be ready to date, but you should probably follow your instincts. But beware, you may still be in the rebound category so behave and choose accordingly. Slow is fine.

Remember the famous scene in *Bound* where Jennifer Tilly goes over to Gina Gershon with those two cups of coffee? An all-time classic of "is it a date or is it just coffee?'" answered definitively. The point: If you don't try, you'll never know.

Under 20

You are *so* not ready to date. But solitude can be a good thing. Still, you may want to reread all the essays in this book to see if you've missed something.

Note: To everyone who took this quiz, remember: "What is yours won't pass you by." I don't know who said that first, but I think they're right. Also: I've been in all three categories—in fact, screwed-up in all three categories—so I hope this test will spare someone else an embarrassing moment (or year).

part two

Dating

The most mysterious and baffling part
of the gay-girl experience.
It's not as scary as you think,
though some of your dates may be.
Be brave, be strong, oh, my sister-woman-sister,
and you might meet...her.

Butch/Femme:
Do You Know Who You Are?

A major resurgence of the butch/femme aesthetic has overtaken the lesbian nation, or more broadly the gay-girl world—which, of course, includes bisexual women and the transgender-identified. At various times in the course of my dating career, I have been pegged as both butch and femme, and I've become fascinated with the implications and possibilities this sensibility can offer. Ho that I am, I want all the babes I can get. But more about that later.

Now, to start with, a brief discussion of what all this means. Since I teach LGBT studies at two colleges, I've researched this phenomenon thoroughly and know one thing: It's wide-open to interpretation and to how each individual defines her own gender or sexual identity. Therefore, this analysis is a compilation of academic research, personal experience, ideas, and explanations from my students, friends, and other LGBT studies professors...and my somewhat off-kilter sense of humor.

Here goes: It's not all about the visuals (haircut, clothes, etc.), though they are handy indicators. It's mostly about an erotic energy that's intertwined with one's personality that includes attitude, sexual desire, worldview, and of course, choice of footgear. (OK, not always the latter, but I don't know any full-on butch who owns a pair of high heels, or a high femme who doesn't own at least five pairs of those sexy yet spinal column–challenging shoes.)

All of the full-on butches (a category I made up, but it's not the same as stone butch, which I'll get to in a second), I know have always felt on the boi-male-gentlemanly side of things. This generally involves having had a childhood of hyper-tomboy behavior and tastes as well as an immediate discomfort or even hatred of wearing the obligatory dress after the age of 5. If you're interested in this topic, Daphne Scholinski's book *The Last Time I Wore a Dress* is a terrific resource, as is Phyllis Burke's *Gender Shock,* which is more of an overview of all things gender and also a great read. Another recommendation is Joan Nestle's classic *The Persistent Desire: A Femme-Butch Reader* and for real fun for the femmes, Shar Rednour's *The Femme's Guide to the Universe* is a hoot as well as very informative.

Now, a common notion about butches is that they want to be men or that their outlook mimics the heterosexual model. But all the butches I know rail against this idea, as they believe there are not just two genders, but numerous genders; for them, it's not about "opposites." That old *binary* war horse: that men and women are "opposites," and the assumption is that everyone is heterosexual and acting accordingly. Yeah, right.

This is also true for the femme-identified women I know: Most of them are not interested in passing for straight or following the het model; they aspire toward a different kind of femininity—not the traditional one we're all so familiar with. As my high-femme-from-birth friend Veronica says, "It isn't that a femme can't do everything a butch can do— sometimes she just chooses not to."

Which brings me to stone butches: women who general-ly can't pass for straight and never have. In addition, the term often refers to lesbians who are "tops" and may not want to be touched sexually. For more on this, read Leslie Feinberg's classic *Stone Butch Blues,* a brilliant autobiographical novel.

At this point, I can't resist throwing in something I heard at a recent LGBT studies conference in New York City: "The joke in the Bay Area is there are no butches anymore— they're all men now." The point, of course, is that many butch women have become, or are in the process of becoming, transsexual FTMs (women who've gone from female to male). This trend may be exclusive to the San Francisco Bay Area. Or maybe the Bay Area is a good place to be, if you want to make that transition between genders.

One of my closest friends, Karla, is a self-acknowledged expert in figuring out a woman's butch/femme status with amazing accuracy. She has taken on yours truly as a special case, one she is determined to crack. Some butches think I'm femme or femme-looking, since I do like to wear makeup and cute shoes and love being on a boi-ish girl's arm. Conversely, some femmes think I'm "boi butch" enough (a subcategory) to qualify as butch, but that could have more to do with my sporty physique and the way I walk and who knows what else? Other femmes see me as one of their own—albeit one who needs a few tips on accessories and whatnot. Therefore, if they only like butches, I'm not in the ballpark, not even in the cheap seats. But I can squeak by with femme-to-femme types, because I don't wear skirts or know what one actually does to cuticles—I do know it has something to do with your nails.

To determine whether I am butch or femme, Karla first looked at my most recent girlfriends. The serious ones. Since we've been friends for more than 10 years, that's pretty much everyone I've ever had a serious relationship with. One was fairly femme (Ann Taylor suits/skirts, Prada shoes, an executive administrator type), and one was fairly butch (a Leonardo DiCaprio look-alike, very androgynous, boots or shoes that lace only, no makeup, professional chef). But this was a dead end that landed me first on one side of the gender spectrum, then the other. Girlfriend # 3, the most recent, was butch-identified but owned this clingy, cute little black dress, which at my request she wore on New Year's Eve. Let's call her "Butch Skirt." This only confused the issue.

Both Great Shoes and Leonardo made their apartments adorable and did most of the cooking. But that led Karla and me nowhere in figuring out my butch-or-femme quotient. Neither decorating ability nor cooking talent is solely a femme or butch trait. It's just that by comparison my efforts in both areas have been uninspired.

Then there was Butch Skirt, who for two years was an LDD (long-distance dating) girlfriend with whom I never cohabited. We mostly traded off or split up the cooking and took turns picking up the check in restaurants. Though I almost always was the one to make the coffee and serve it to her in bed. Some might see this as a femme quality, though a gentleman butch surely might be the one to pop up out of the warmth to let her femme doze a bit longer. Others might see it for the caffeine control freak that I am (I travel with my own blend).

Not one of these details is a hard-and-fast indicator; one must look at the whole picture, according to Karla. In fact, Great Shoes could spend every Saturday afternoon at Home Depot—the lesbian emporium for the married crowd. And Leonardo always changed the oil in the car. Of course, I'd date any butch just to avoid that nasty job. This might be a femme indictor, but more than likely it's a lazy "I don't like to get my fingernails gross" indicator. Though that in fact may be a femme indicator (not the laziness, the nail care aspect).

Then, as truly enigmatic as I am myself is Butch Skirt, a scientist who loved figuring out how things worked and put together all of my IKEA furniture in 30 minutes or less. You know, IKEA's that place that packs only one L-wrench thing to build apparently anything. You say you want to build the Taj Mahal? All you'll need is an L-wrench. Good thing Butch Skirt came equipped with power tools. I, on the other hand, am afraid of drills and such. They might jump out of my hand and give me an impromptu lobotomy.

Still unable to determine my status, Karla asked who got to keep the apartment after each breakup (the femme *always* gets the apartment). But I was one for one there too, though this was somewhat consistent with Karla's theory: Great Shoes (vaguely more femme than yours truly) got our apartment, and I got the place I'd shared with Leonardo. I never lived with Butch Skirt, so it's a draw. Now, since my last significant breakup, I've dated a variety of women, one of whom was a full-on butch. Thus, Karla insisted on giving me femme lessons, of which I was apparently in desperate need.

According to Karla, it's all about cars. First, a femme is

never to open her own car door (you can bet she won't be driving either). The butch opens the door, then closes it after the femme is neatly tucked in (you may have seen your parents do this when you were a kid). If you are the femme, you are to stare blankly but beautifully into the night. Do not even think of picking up the dinner check; that's insulting—especially during the courtship phase.

This particular butch I dated had some major control issues—like when I was allowed to talk. Wrong girl for me—in a big way. So I'm still not exactly sure whether I'm femme enough for a full-on butch. I know I'd like to try being femme enough anyway, since pheromones can strike you anytime.

To close: Explore! Have fun and have sex and find out what works for you. I dubbed my friend Lynnly a whimsical butch and it stuck. There are as many genders/identifications out there as you can imagine. For now, I've decided to identify (for shorthand) as a femme-tomboi or tomboi-femme. Of course, that's today, anyway. And there are so many other gender types one can be on any given day. Oh, and Karla claims I am her one and only unsolved case. I feel honored.

Honestly Dating

I've noticed an alarming trend in gay-girl dating: honesty. Not the kind of honesty that makes you a stand-up person who pays your bills on time and never gossips maliciously. I'm talking about an entirely different strain. It's the type of frankness that makes me think, *I never, even in my most voyeuristic moment, wanted to know that about you. What possessed you to think I'd be interested in that bizarre/salacious/way-too-intimate detail from your life?*

Take the too honest first date. Or, as I like to call it, the "vomiting up your entire wretched- past before dessert" date. You know, when you've barely ordered the bruschetta and she says, "So, my ex cheated on me after we were together for three years—with MY EX from college! I can't tell you how betrayed and abandoned I felt." *Please,* I silently scream, *don't tell me.* I listen in horror and wonder, if I go to the bathroom and never come back, how abandoned would she feel then? But that would be so rude, so I stay put, transfixed. Then she announces, "I wish you hadn't worn blue. It reminds me of my ex—she always wore blue." I ask myself how one gets through life avoiding the color blue.

She continues, my blue shirt notwithstanding, "So at the same time my ex dumped me, my cat got this weird feline lupus-like leukemia—are you going to finish your salad? Anyway, she's got this puss coming out of her eyes—my cat, not my ex…"

Why is she telling me all this? Either I'm better at controlling my expression than I used to be or this woman is truly oblivious. This is TOO much honesty. What happened to the art of conversation? Witty repartee? Current events, for God's sake? Let's talk about movies, books, the waiter's haircut. Anything but this.

Then there's the "I've had too much therapy" kind of honesty. I was once on a second or third date, and the conversation went something like this.

Date: "I want you to know that I'm not emotionally available at all since my breakup. And I'll probably only be sexually available for the first month or two—that's when my trust issues come up."

Me: "When did your relationship end?"

Date: "Seven years ago."

Now, there's information you can use.

Don't get me wrong—some honesty is a good thing. Like when my date, an hour late, explains, "I'm so sorry, but I got pulled over and my car was impounded because I'm driving on a suspended license because of my last DUI. Hey, can I get you a drink? I sure could use one." I'm glad I've learned I'm on a date with a junior alcoholic and thus will act accordingly. Do I end the date by stopping at a 12-step meeting or do I politely tell her, "Gosh, I think we're too different. I like to be conscious and you...don't."

Before you get the impression that all my dates do this, I want to assure you there are plenty of relatively normal, interesting women out there—many of whom wait months to tell me their last names. Nonetheless, too much up-front honesty is a frightening trend in the lezzie dating world. I mean, there's a big difference between blatant disclosure and honesty; as far as I'm concerned, just because it's the truth, I don't necessarily want to hear it. Of course, if you've got a funny story about how you ran into Gina Gershon at a fund-raiser where her sexy outfit got tangled up and you got to be the disentangler—that I'd like to hear about.

Top 10 Things Not to Say on a First Date

10. I've got this weird rash on my back—can you look?

9. Sorry I'm late—I was bleaching my mustache.

8. I'm telling you, those Kegel exercises have changed my life.

7. God, my underwear is *so* riding up my butt.

6. Be right back, gotta call home so Mom doesn't worry.

5. Do you have any Midol? I am *so-o-o* bloated.

4. I've taken a vow of celibacy—and you?

3. Does everyone in your family have those funny ears?

2. I'm clean out of Prozac. Got any? Paxil or Zoloft are fine too.

1. When was the last time you had your teeth cleaned? Looks like someone's due…

The Daisy Chain of Ex-lovers of Ex-lovers

Envision the '70s kids game Barrel of Monkeys, the object of which is to hook as many tiny plastic monkeys together in the longest chain possible. Now you have the visual image of the labyrinthine cross index of lovers and ex-lovers in any lesbian community—from San Francisco to Pocatello.

I came out in Chico, California, in the mid '80s during my freshman or sophomore year of college. I can't quite remember the exact year because those kinds of distinctions hardly mattered in the no-ambition "let's party" days of the '80s. It didn't, however, take me long to figure out that no matter whom I dated, I probably knew, had heard of, or was friends with one of her exes. This unnerved me. I imagined clandestine meetings where the new lover talked with the ex-lover, comparing notes about me and discussing strategies. OK, maybe it was all the pot I smoked back then. But still, this phenomena can't be nearly as prevalent in the world of straight dating.

There's something creepy to me about having two people who've known me in the biblical sense (and more), and now they're doing the wild thing together. You know it'll come up at some point. I've never done it, so I can't be sure about this, but I'm guessing that at some point they've got to dish about me. Let's face it, the girls get chatty once they're post-coital. What resounds in my head goes something like this:

40

"She did that with YOU!? She wouldn't with me…" From there, I imagine that every detail of the "love" we shared will be *shared* by both of my exes. It's like one big lesbian loop of love that eventually you'll end up at the beginning with your first lover and on and on. OK, that's the totally paranoid nightmare scenario—and also one of the reasons I moved to San Francisco: more gay girls, less comparing of notes.

Recently, I went to a gay-girl event with my friend Chris, whereupon I realized that in our row of seats, out of seven women, I was the only one who wasn't one of Chris's ex-lovers. All of Chris's exes had become her close friends after the breakup. Which makes for a fertile breeding ground for them to meet, greet, and sleep with each other (think petri dish). I, on the other hand, have never stayed close friends with any of my ex-lovers.

In the lesbian nation this would indicate I need therapeutic help. In the straight community, I find, exes are people you occasionally run into in at some social function. When you break it off with your boyfriend or girlfriend, you don't start making weekly brunch dates. To me, this makes sense. When you break up with someone, it's for a reason. That's not to say that at some point you might not become friends, but a year or five in the future.

I did have one daisy-chain experience some years ago. I was just getting my start as a comic and briefly dated a beautiful woman we'll call Jane. One night we were out together and ran into a headlining comic friend of mine and I introduced them.

A few months after Jane and I had stopped dating, we had lunch together. The following conversation ensued:

Jane: "I've been seeing someone."

Me: "That's good."

Jane: "It's someone you know, actually."

Me: "Really? Who?"

She named the headlining comic.

Without skipping a beat I replied: "Who's next, Ellen DeGeneres?"

Jane was horrified. Well, I say, if you're going to sleep your way up the lesbian-comic ladder, you have to expect a snide comment or two.

So why do so many gay girls date/have relationships with their friends' exes? Is it simply because we have a smaller playing field—we are after all only 5% of the population. Or is it some tribal instinct? By that, I mean you're an athletic sort, so you tend to date other athletes. Eventually, two of your exes will be on the same soccer team...and you know the rest. The same could be said for political activists, corporate climbers, or arty intellectuals. But still, why such consistency of taste? Could it be true that we're all dating the same person over and over again until we get it right? Now I've made myself crazy.

I'm still not sure why so many gay girls hunt in the same grounds. Conversely, there is definitely something to be said for variety. Hopefully, it won't be the same girl/different haircut.

Top 10 Things Not to Wear on a First Date

10. Anything with fringe.

9. Any kind of athletic gear, unless you're going rock climbing or scuba diving.

8. Any T-shirt with writing on it (especially one that says, MY GIRLFRIEND WENT TO HAWAII AND ALL I GOT WAS THIS LOUSY T-SHIRT).

7. Anything so tight that after one deep breath half of your outfit is airborne.

6. Anything so comfortable it makes you look like you just rolled out of bed.

5. A completely monochromatic outfit (with, of course, the exception of all black).

4. Sloppy footgear. It's just plain wrong.

3. Undergarments that show on purpose—unless you're not really interested in the talking part anyway.

2. A hood over your head, unless it's extremely cold and you don't end up looking like a Smurf.

1. Jagged or unmanicured nails. Nothing says I can take or leave this date louder.

Blind Dates: Think Hunters and Ducks

Has anyone ever had a successful blind date? By that I mean have you ever actually gotten to the end of the evening without fantasizing about how much fun you'd have when you got home and flossed your teeth? Friends who set us up mean well—they honestly do. But I've been on a few blind dates that make me question what my friends really think of me—or if they even know me at all.

For gay girls, it's our straight friends and gay men who set us up on actual meet-you-at-a-restaurant-type blind dates. Our female friends plan an entire event to get the lucky couple together. This inevitably involves food, sports, or watching sports while eating food. In my experience, there are two basic techniques employed in setting up blind dates.

Technique 1 occurs when whoever sets you up goes on and on about how gorgeous and smart and charming your potential date is. They go to great pains to explain that a catch like her won't be single long, so you'd better jump on it (or on her, whichever comes first). This technique almost always proves that beauty is in the eye of the beholder, and unfortunately it's not your eye.

For example, I was once invited to a small soiree to meet a friend's single friend whom she said I was "just going to love!" Not only was it not my particular eye that was going to behold her beauty, but she never said a word throughout the entire dinner beyond "Yes," "No," and "Thank you." Truly.

The next day the matchmaker called me to ask, "So what do you think?"

"About what?" I said.

"Sheri, silly! She really liked you!"

"She didn't say a word to me," I countered.

"Sometimes she gets shy in crowds," the matchmaker said.

Crowds? There were six of us.

What was my friend thinking? That I'd do the talking for both of us? No, thank you. I've spent 10 years on stage as a stand-up comedienne, essentially talking to myself for money. I won't do it for free.

Technique 2 is employed when your friends invite you to a casual Friday night dinner, then coyly announce, "Oh, Mo, have you met Denise? She works with Robin?" Although my face and voice offer the usual polite pleasantries, my brain screams, *Get me out of here!* Plus, I'm always hideously self-conscious about not having changed out of the T-shirt I dribbled coffee down the front of moments before I left home. This woman may not be my dream date, but looking like a unkempt slob won't make me her dream date either. Knowing I'm a champ at social denial of all sorts, my friends can trust me to be conversant and charming toward the woman (after all, it's not her fault), but I'll be plotting revenge on the inside (it *is* my friends' fault). That's another handy trick I gleaned from comedy—talking and appearing attentive while having a whole other conversation in my head. It's a truly invaluable blind-date skill.

A gay man I know once set up an extremely attractive, witty friend of mine with a woman he rhapsodized about. He said she was "gorgeous, petite, blond, loaded with personality, and very successful in business." Not only was the woman quite homely (I saw her myself), but she was way beyond petite—more like the anorexic "please drink a milk shake" type. Appearances aside, she talked nonstop through the entire dinner about her job and only her job. My friend now knows more about managing a group of systems analysts than anybody's business, and she told me she was so exhausted after the date that she felt like she had run a marathon and was then hit by a Mack truck. To add insult to injury, the woman called her the very next day for a second date. She never even noticed my friend's "I give up" silence or lack of "pheromonal" response." It does give one pause.

Given the mismatching of 95% of all blind dates, a girl's got to have some escape-route strategies. There's the tried and true method of straight-up telling them you have tickets to a show after dinner. This gives you a time frame you can work with, no matter how stilted the conversation is. But no matter what, it's inexcusable to tell her you'll take care of the check, but once you're up at the register and you've got that distance between you, you flee the scene (though you did pay the check). That's in very bad form, no matter how loudly she slurped her soup.

For those just fresh from a grueling blind date, I offer this tasty tidbit from my dating history.

The Long Dark Date

I drive calmly through the rain-soaked streets of San Francisco. Traffic lights and expensive shoes reflect off the slick surface. I look at my watch: 7:10. I relax my tendency to put too much pedal to the metal. No tickets tonight, officer, not for some babe my friend Robin set me up with. Robin who's been married so long she figures anyone with an IQ over 60 and a pulse is good enough for me—that is, given my track record. Hey, how was I supposed to know she had a personality disorder? I thought she was just extra moody. And one of those personalities was great in bed. Time is taking its time as I look again: 7:13. Why don't they make these red light stops longer? A girl could get some real thinking done. Who knew one of her personalities simply couldn't let go? There's only so long that even I can stand being stalked. Yeah, it wasn't pretty, but so much of life on the Barbary Coast is like that (not pretty).

I approach the meeting place cautiously. Some hoo-ha eatery that opened after the dot-commers and their ilk left town. No more $125-a-plate restaurants in this neighborhood. I remember when you couldn't keep a restaurant open down here that charged more than $5.95 a plate and included salad. Sure, it was iceberg lettuce, maybe a chick pea or two slipped in for color, but salad nonetheless. I remember too much these days. Five years is a long time in this town. You can barely turn around without some babe or bouncer spitting olives at you. Olives, California grows a lot of olives. But Frisco, she's the town I love. Probably grow old here, if I get the chance. Damn, I wanted to be early so I could scope out a good seat, but now it's 7:25 and I still haven't found a parking space. This Impala might be old, but she's as dependable as the mayor lying to us.

I park parallel, figuring I'll start a trend on this street. People are like that in this town: Give 'em any reason to park and they'll line up. I slip out the passenger side, since Miss

Personality permanently dented my driver's side. Thanks for the souvenir, kid. I spot my "date" at the window seat, just like Robin said, medium brown hair and a body like Pamela Lee (before the implants—I like my women natural). She could be trouble. I circle the restaurant, checking for escape routes (and exes with a bad case of PMS and proximity to olives). I'm making a second pass when she spots me. She beckons me over with a wave and a smile that could light Vegas. Wonder how Robin described me? Thirties, messy color-of-the-week hair cut short, an affection for plaid hip-huggers? And she'd be right, except that tonight I'm sporting little round glasses instead of contacts—a girl's got to live it up occasionally. I try not to be too impressed as I walk to the table. She seems almost normal. There's gotta be a catch. There's always a catch in this town. I sit. Not one for small talk, I ask her what she does.

"For what?" she slyly asks, as she seductively breaks off a piece of bread.

"Work?" I venture, not to be won over that easy. I've seen the bread trick before.

"Graphic design." She chews with meaning.

"That's too bad." Everyone in town knows graphic designers are a dime, not even a quarter, a dozen these days.

"Not so bad—I wasn't working for a start-up. Strictly corporate." Her knife plays with the half-empty butter dish.

"Tell me more." Two can play at this game, sister. I make birdlike shapes with my napkin.

"Not much to tell," she says. "My mother was a graphics person and her mother before her. Guess it runs in the gene pool." She motions to the server. I like a woman who takes control. This

could get interesting. Not that many women can flag down a waiter faster than it takes to recite the specials of the day. She's confident, good-looking—there has to be a catch. And there is.

"So that's how you hooked up with Robin—it's getting clearer, maybe too clear." I add the last part so it doesn't sound like small talk.

"Let's get to it, Miz Mo, you into water sports or what?" Her stare makes tunnels where my eyes once were.

"You mean like surfing, boogie boarding, jet skiing, or...the other?" I decisively swallow a mouthful of dry sourdough bread. Why is it always sourdough? A nice corn rye occasionally wouldn't hurt this town.

"The other..." Her unbroken stare bears down on me without mercy. Does she know my weakness? Does it show?

"You mean..?" I grab for my water and gulp.

"Yes, water pistols, water balloons...you name it." She's won. I can't resist a good water balloon fight. Not since I was a child. How did she know? Where would all this end?

I didn't know what would happen, but I did know I'd play. I had to. Like her, it was in my gene pool. This long dark date would last the entire weekend. Fool that I was. I thought it was all in good fun. But there's not such thing as good clean fun. Not in this town. Not in my life.

And with that I close tonight's episode of The Long Dark Date. Stay tuned...

Parody aside, if you're game, blind dates can actually work out. We all know people who've met and fallen in love through friends. Those stories seem to take on mythic proportions.

Still, bravo for them. I haven't been one of those charmed people. I'm not sure why—maybe it really *is* all planetary alignment. Oh, and my apologies to any serious Dashiell Hammett/Raymond Chandler fans.

Where the Girls Are

One place you might consider: the gym. Sure, it's a stereotype that many gay girls are sporty types. Mostly because it's true. Therefore, the gym is an excellent place to meet or at least see other gay girls, and you might even enjoy the rush of endorphins while you're at it.

It's clear to me that a lot of single people view the gym as a good place to meet other single people—otherwise why would everyone be so dressed up? Don't get me started on women, gay or straight, who wear lipstick at the gym. That is just plain wrong. Lip gloss, maybe; a bit of light lip polish or Chapstick, definitely; but lip-lined dark full-color glossy model-from-an-ad lipstick has no place in the gym. OK, that's just me.

One can generally pick out the gay girls because of their gym outfits. Generally, this would mean loose but expensive sweatpants, a tank top, and a zip or pullover sweatshirt. The sweatshirt comes off in 10 minutes and is subsequently carried around and used as a towel. Gay girls have been known to break a sweat. Plus, those hard worked-for biceps, triceps, and delts deserve their day in the sun...or fluorescence. There's also the long (to the knee) nylon shorts and athletic shoe look, as well as the occasional black spandex tights. And all gay girls wear full armor athletic bras—big or small, we want those puppies strapped down but good.

The black spandex leotards are generally seen on two types of women, gay or straight: trainers/bodybuilders (think visibly muscular butts) and women who believe that black is slimming and are in denial about what spandex can do to one's thighs and butt. How they remain in denial is beyond me, as the gym is lined with floor-to-ceiling mirrors. There is one particularly odd look for women that I don't think is a gay-girl thing: the black "spandex full-body leotard with a neon pink, green, or yellow triangle flap over the pelvis region in front G-string up the butt" look. What is this? A signaling device? Maybe it helps them locate body parts in that sea of black spandex: "If this is my pelvis, these must be my legs…"

Knowing of my gym addiction, my sister, whom I adore, decided to get me a new gym outfit for my birthday—a full-on periwinkle spandex outfit. I thanked her and figured I could wear it under my baggy nylon shorts—maybe. She had me try it on; I felt naked and color-coded. No matter how fit I get, I don't think I'll ever feel confident in a sausage casing.

But I am impressed with how great some people's outfits are at the gym—possibly because I constantly fall so short in that category. For three years now, I've been wearing the same blue or gray bleach-and-paint-splattered sweatpants and T-shirts they give away at Gay Pride events or mall openings. I'm all class.

Trying to fight your body's natural inclination to droop is tough work and tougher if you reward yourself with a Big Mac. Therefore, the juice and smoothie places (other gay-girl hangouts) have lines out the door as solid food is replaced with wheat grass, bee pollen, or soy protein shakes. I do this occasionally for lunch on the run, but by 4 P.M. I'm unfit to drive. My hunger pangs have convinced me that no one else should even attempt to be in my lane. So let this be a warning to those prone to road rage—eat a real sandwich, hold the mayo, and call it health food.

All in all, there's really there's no way to lose at the gym. Even if you don't meet anyone you click with, you'll feel and look better when you do. A footnote: At my gym both the men's and women's locker rooms post large signs over the sauna that say: SEXUAL ACTIVITY STRICTLY PROHIBITED. ANYONE CAUGHT WILL BE IMMEDIATELY EXPELLED AND WILL LOSE THEIR GYM MEMBERSHIP! In California, losing one's gym membership is like getting court-martialed. I've gone to gyms around the country and only in San Francisco do they have to tell the women they can't have sex in the locker rooms.

Another great way to meet other gay girls is by taking a class—especially in women's studies or the emerging field of LGBT studies. I teach in both fields at two colleges, and it's clear to me that the classroom setting is ripe with dating opportunities. The really cool thing about teaching is that you get to think and talk about all of these interesting ideas while simultaneously checking out the babe quotient.

The age range of my students differs greatly, depending on whether I'm teaching during the day or at night. My day classes heavily favor 20-somethings; people in my night classes range from being right out of high school to senior citizens.

Every semester I watch the chessboard-like moves of women who start at the back of the class but over the course of the semester move closer, inch by inch, row by row, to the object of their affections. By the time finals roll around, if it's a go, happy lovers are sitting side by side, leaning over and writing in each other's notebooks and giggling over private jokes. I always find this so charming, unless of course I've been single for a long stretch, in which case, I wish I were taking the class, not teaching it.

Without fail, at least three to four new couples emerge by the end of the course. I love the idea that radical intellectual discourse can bring about love connections, but I know from experience that more than likely it's just matching pheromones placed in proximity to each other.

Another longtime favorite: the gay-girl bookstore/café. Now, they don't always come with a café. though many do— how else are you going to be able to ask if they mind sharing the table? The cafés are traditionally small enough so that there's almost always a table shortage, hence increasing your chances of talking to the woman who just bought *Herotica 1, 2,* and *3.* This gay girl is definitely single, and from the looks of it, it's been a while. This is not a time to get shy. You *did* catch her looking at you in the queer theory section, remember? Even if she didn't, sharing a table is not a long-term commitment. Lest you bother a completely uninterested stranger, since you made the first move, sit, smile, and sip your latte. If she finds something to comment on, like your book, the virtues of soy chai, how uncomfortable the chairs are (a given), you might actually be on your way to meeting someone new.

On the other hand, if she's flipping through *How to Communicate With Your Partner,* skip that table. This woman's for sure struggling to prolong a rocky relationship, and if she's the "talk to anyone" type, you might be in for the long haul. Or she may your next non-girlfriend girlfriend, since she's so cute and she *is* in an open relationship—well, sort of. Cut your losses now and move on to a table where someone is reading, say, *Is It a Date or Just Coffee?* This would show she has exquisite taste and/or likes to laugh (how could I resist?).

The longest standing tradition, other than the military, is of course the local softball team. Being a gifted athlete is not required, since who cares, being sisters, even if you're warming the bench and only get to play when the teams either winning or losing by 10? Plus, you'll get some exercise, meets tons of women, and it's fun. I have to admit that I've never been good at softball—basketball, yes, even coached, but since I'm left-handed, I somehow never caught on to the throwing part (that's the official excuse). The few times I did play, I was literally put in left field. Still, I felt curiously at home out there. I could catch anything, but if it was a grounder, the shortstop would haul ass toward me in an effort to shorten the distance I'd have to throw. And they *still* kept me. Other sports with a high gay-girl ratio are basketball, field hockey, rugby, and flag football—especially field hockey. If you played field hockey in high school, there was a 50/50 chance you'd be a gay girl. If you were captain of the team, you can skip that bisexual stage, you're a dyke. Not to diss my bi sisters, but some gay girls simply don't have that "men can be fun too" gene.

Now, the rugby girls have always intrigued but vaguely frightened me—those scrimmage-huddle things are way too much body contact for this girl. Then there's all that mud. In some ways it looks fun—like when you were a kid and being mud encrusted was the norm. Still, you do get to tackle the girl with the ball, and that might have its advantages.

The sport that has taken off like wildfire in the last 10 years or so is women's flag football. In Key West, there is in fact the Kelly McGillis International Women's and Girls' Flag Football Championship, held annually in February. Sixty-five teams from eight countries. I mean, who wouldn't want to go to Key West in February, a month so miserable that they had to shave off a few days? Though not an exclusively gay-girl event, there are gay girls aplenty and from as far away as Sweden. I know, because in the 2002 tournee I somehow ended up being both the comic entertainment and the grand marshal of the parade (yes, there's a parade—how Key West of them!). A good, raucous time was had by all. Those footballers like to party.

Another great way to meet other gay girls is by getting involved with a local queer political or nonprofit organization. They always need volunteers, no matter what kind of skills you have or don't have. I find I'm exceptional at stuffing and collating envelopes. I'm also good at picking up the pizzas or running for emergency espressos. And even if you don't meet the woman of your dreams (or even a date), it'll make you feel good.

Oddly, I failed to mention the local gay bar. Probably because I've never met anyone I'd seriously date at a club or bar. Sure, I've collected my share of phone numbers, but the next day it's simply not as great an idea as it was the night before. Between the music, the lighting (or lack thereof), and a couple of cocktails, you really have no idea what inspired you to ask for her number (or give out yours). If you must go to a bar to meet women, I say go with your running buddies, have no expectations, and who knows? Incidentally, it's my theory that you meet the most women at clubs waiting for the bathroom, and since gay girls love to line up, that might be your best shot.

Closing footnote: If you're getting a bit blue about your single status, stay away from Home Depot on the weekends. It becomes a lesbian couple emporium. Pick up the power tool another time.

Top 10 Reasons Date #2 Will Take Place in Hell or Prison

10. Your date tongue-kisses the cute butch bouncer at the dance club so the two of you can hop the line. She offers no explanation. You wonder how she'll pay for a round of drinks.

9. An hour into your date, you realize you dated her sister in college and suddenly see the family resemblance. You fight the gag reflex.

8. At the local queer-trendy restaurant, you are happily eating tiny overpriced appetizers when you catch her exchanging glances with a woman who turns out to be her ex. You resist the urge to hurl the last of the ginger-aioli crabcakes at her.

7. During your good-night kiss, someone drives up and takes a flashbulb picture and drives off. Your date says nothing, as though it's a common occurrence.

6. When you come back from the restroom, she's seated with her coat fully buttoned and her bag on her shoulder. Then she excuses herself to the restroom. As soon as she's out of sight, you check for your wallet.

5. She starts every third sentence with "Don't take this the wrong way, but…" You decide to take it any way you feel like and wish you were home eating ice cream and watching the Weather Channel.

4. She insists on going to an out-of-town restaurant, then explains she has a very jealous almost ex-boyfriend who just got out on probation. Your response: "Check, please."

3. During a romantic post-dinner walk, she explains how all her meds have been straightened out. And that stalking thing? For sure, that won't happen again—*really.*

2. Your fetching though "young-looking for a 27-year-old" date admits that actually she's not quite out of high school and still lives with her Pentecostal parents.

1. After a great kiss good night, while still in your embrace your date whispers that you are *so* like her ex and she has this great outfit she'd love for you to wear. In public. (Think Hitchcock's *Vertigo.*)

The Non-date Date

Many of us have experienced this ambiguous state of affairs (pun unintended...oh, make it intended): the non-date date. This phenomenon occurs when you've been doing a lot of "palling" around with a new or old friend/acquaintance, and it's so laden with sexual innuendo you'd need a forklift to get to the bottom of it. But trust me, with the non-date date you will never get to the bottom of it because nothing definitive *ever* happens. Except that you start to doubt your grasp of reality, *and* still you keep hanging out with said person. Why? If I knew, I wouldn't be writing this in angst and bewilderment and from more personal experience than I will ever admit to.

First, this caveat: If you are currently having problems with untempered projection or delusions, or have been single so long that you read sexual innuendo into the most benign situations, this essay is not for you. You can test yourself right now. If anytime in the last month or so, the phrase "Paper or plastic?" sounded flirtatious, then you're probably imagining things of a sexual nature with your NDD (non-date date) and everyone else for that matter. Think about seeking professional help. However, if you don't fall into any of the above categories, then I guarantee it—you are not in fact imagining anything. And that's the problem.

There are a few prerequisites to creating this situation; generally one of you is single and the other is either recently single or going through one of those eternal on-again/off-again breakups. You can both be single, but there's usually something in the realm of romance that's going on with one of you that encourages the sexual energy to go all over the place. It is literally filling up and spilling over, with or without you or your NDD's cognitive awareness. (I have to throw in a big word occasionally; it rationalizes those 10 years in grad school and the fact that I am owned lock, stock, and barrel by Sallie Mae, that she-devil of school loans.)

I know about NDD because I've been on both sides of it. Whenever I've been the playful but still entangled person, I've been mostly oblivious to the amount of flirtatious/ sexual charge I'm either getting from or giving to my "friend." I might later think, *God, I hope she didn't take that the wrong way.* But that's as much time as I'd give the thought, especially if I was embroiled in a messy romantic thing of one sort or another (you may use your imagination here). Frankly, I didn't realize I'd done this to someone until she called me on it. I was stunned. Of course, I denied it initially, mostly because it was such a creepy thing to do. Eventually, I did admit to myself—and weeks later to her— that there was a certain flirty thing going on, I guess, during that stressful time. But hey, no big deal—we didn't act on it, right? I mean, we're friends, after all, yes? I felt way lame, as I should have.

Being on the other side of an NDD is worse. It proves that ignorance is bliss. Allow me to illustrate: Let's say you're at the movies with your NDD, and suddenly the proximity is either too close, too far, or altogether way too self-conscious. You keep telling yourself, *This is a no-brainer; she's a friend, so what's the diff?*—that is, if you talk to yourself in outdated slang). You settle in once more, get into the movie, and there it is AGAIN: *Is her shoulder touching mine on purpose? Do I even notice this with my other friends? Are the theater seats getting smaller? Am I getting larger?* OK, maybe not that last one, unless you're young enough to still be in a growing cycle, in which case this book is not for you. So again you lean away to solve the dilemma and try to focus on the movie. You adore Jennifer Jason Leigh/Brendan Fraser/Helen Hunt in anything—why can't you go to "movie head"? At this point it may start to annoy you; for nine bucks you should know whether you're on a date or not.

Now, if your new constant pal is ending an LTR that numbers over five years, there's a better-than-even chance that she hasn't had sex in the last six months to four years, hence the sexual innuendo that oozes through the cracks and crevices of otherwise innocent comments.

For instance, I walked right by my NDD at a drag king show where I was supposed to meet her. When she asked how I'd missed her, given that I'd passed her within inches, I quipped something like this, hoping to underscore the friendship of it all: "I didn't have time to throw in my contacts, and since I think I look cuter without glasses, I didn't want to walk in with them on. See, the woman of my dreams might be here, and I want to look good."

"The glasses are good—really cute," she said as her neck went scarlet.

I couldn't help but notice this, so I went into my joke mode: "Of course, if I can't see the woman of my dreams, that would defeat the whole purpose…"

"You walked right by me..." she repeated.

I stared off, scanning the crowd with my glasses on, supposedly for that elusive woman of my dreams. Now, the NDD may have meant those comments in a positive, friendly way, and the blushing neck thing? Well, who knows?

Does your NDD know she's flirting or at least giving that impression? At best, there's only a 50/50 chance of that being true, because denial forms a large part of how the NDD syndrome works. Now, I have to say in all fairness that the NDD is usually not malicious and you're usually a willing participant for some reason. Also, at some level I think we all know when we're flirting or giving off that vibe. When we choose to acknowledge this is completely arbitrary, and some people will never admit it—ever. And it never, and I mean never, actually goes anywhere romantic, because let's face it, it was some kind of temporary fix for one or both parties. Once that need is over, it sort of wears itself out. To qualify: If the flirting does go anywhere romantic, it's a short ride to hell. So just be grateful that (a) you were not delusional; (b) the NDD experience motivated you to get out there and find a *real* date; (c) thank God nothing ever happened, because now you'd feel like a true idiot; and (d) with any luck at all, you'll get your friend back—as a friend only.

I'm Not a Baby Dyke. I'm 22 and a Half!

Ah, youth—so much enthusiasm, so much to discover, that first true love…all that not-yet-ruined romantic optimism. You've still got skin unmarked by nothing more than a scattering of post-teen blemishes. Granted, to this day I still break out when I'm PMS-ing. I asked my mother about this pimple thing back in high school. First, she said it would all clear up after college. After college, I asked again. She said it would disappear as soon as I had my first baby. I remember staring at her at the ripe old age of 24 and thinking, *I'm not that desperate to have clear skin.* Fortunately, my brother is still a practicing Catholic—Me? I've got it down, thank you—and had a slew of children, which went a long way toward taking the pressure off me, lesbian or not. But I digress.

Being in the over-30 crowd, my but things have changed. My first teenage inklings of my gay-girl leanings were wrought with shame, confusion, and a lot of bad wine that my best friend and I would drink by the half gallon and then make out and never speak about it. We were 16 years old, and she had a boyfriend and plenty of carnal knowledge of the heterosexual sort. And we were not prepubescent kids: I was talking to a baby dyke recently and asked her where she meets other gay girls. She replied, "Oh, work, school, my mom introduces us—whatever." "Your *mom* introduces you?" Immediately, I realized I was starting to sound like my parents: *In my day you had to get good and drunk to find out you were a lesbian! We'd walk 10 miles in the snow, without shoes to get to that lesbian bar! And when we got there we'd take ANYBODY. She might be the last damn lesbian we'd ever see, and we wanted her! That's because in that one gay bar, there'd be 900 gay men and, like, six lesbians—and they'd all had each other...twice. So we just picked one, had done with it, and were grateful for what we got!*

If you are a baby dyke, you are young and hopefully loving it. You came out post-Ellen, k.d., and Melissa. If you were in the San Francisco Bay Area, you probably took your girlfriend to the prom. Even money says you both wore tuxes just to piss people off and had a grand time of it. The world of women is new and exciting. All of this is a good thing. Though, being painphobic, if I were 19 and came out today, I'd have some tougher choices to make regarding visible *Yes, I'm queer!* coding. I speak of tattoos that start on your neck and wrap around your waist. On someone else, I think many tattoos are quite beautiful, but I can't help inwardly cringing at how much it must have hurt to get done. As much as some heavily tattooed people I know have tried to convince me that the pain of tattooing becomes pleasurable, this girl ain't buying. They don't realize they're talking to someone who doesn't even have her ears pierced, let alone nose, tongue, and various other body parts. I must admit, tongue piercings look very sexy, but I'll stay in the audience, thank you.

When I came out, it was all about haircuts and the pants of the season. I distinctly remember the Z-Cavarricci period, which died a quick death once the suburban mom on *thirtysomething* started wearing them. Once a look leaks to suburbia, whatever the style, it ceases to be a queer clothing code—my point being that the markers when I came out were less…permanent. Tattoos are forever. And once you put a whole in you earlobe a hamster could jump through, there's no going back. Still, I admire anybody's confidence or lack of worry about how their tattoo will look in 20 years. Who cares? It's fabulous *now.*

On to the dating aspect: What I'm focusing on here is the sheer brazenness of the 22-year-old ardently pursuing the older woman—that would be anyone, say, over 32. Not that 32 is old, but in relation to a 22-year-old it is. I remember telling a friend I felt so old, and she asked my age. "Thirty-three," I told her. "You're a baby!" she chuckled. "Well, this is the oldest I've ever been," I said, "and it feels old!" Obviously, age depends on your vantage point.

One couple I know began their relationship when my friend was a mere 27 and her lover was 44: a 17-year age difference. They've been together more than 10 years now, and according to my friend, they still get frisky every weekend. That said, I am now old enough to have had my own affairs on both ends of the spectrum and know its wild sexy appeal and its downside.

When I was a true baby dyke of 19, I went after one of my professors who was 38. I loved the symmetry of it—exactly half or double, depending on how you looked at it. I had to convince her I was exceptionally charming and mature for my age, and quite frankly I was relentless. She just *had* to like me. I was pretty sure she was interested but would never ask me out (some kind of professor ethics thing). But I was a full-on grown-up paying my own rent and everything. So what was the problem, besides this totally arbitrary social construct of "age"?

I finally had my way, and we had a sweet two-month affair. It ended when she went off to France on sabbatical to write her next theoretical-type book. In French *and* English. I thought that was so cool and very sexy. Actually, I still do. Some things don't change, I guess.

The point is, I had no problem whatsoever with the age difference because, well, who cares? Especially when you're 19. Curiously, I totally forgot all about this affair when I was finally old enough to be the older woman and a 22-year-old asked me out. I fumbled and sputtered; our conversation went roughly like this:

Me: I don't know how old you are exactly, but I'm guessing early 20s, and ummm, well, I'm a lot older than you...so I don't think it's a good idea for us to date.

Her: Are you dating someone else?

Me: No.

Her: Would you say yes if I were 10 years older?

Me: Is this a trick question?

Her: No—just tell me the truth.

I couldn't lie, she was exactly my type: all personality, brains, muscles, no money, and too cute.

Me: I guess so.

Her: Then what's the big deal with the age thing?

Me: I...well...it's like we're at different points in our lives and—

Her: Is it because you don't want other people to see you dating me?

Me: It's sort hard to explain—we have totally different...I don't know...references...

Her: What does that mean? Just because we don't listen to the same music we shouldn't date?"

Me: No...not exactly...

Her: It's the "other people" thing. You don't seem like the type of person who would care that much about what other people thought.

She had me there—that *was* one of the bigger reasons. I didn't want my friends to think I couldn't find someone my own age to play with—especially since at the time my last significant lover had been seven years younger than me. When we broke up, I vowed never to date anyone younger than me again. But I couldn't tell this young woman that.

Me: I don't care *that* much what people think—OK, maybe a little.

Her: And it's, like, none of their business—*I'm* dating you, they're not. If you don't like me or if...or if you're not attracted to me, that's different. I'll go away.

Me: I do like you...and you're definitely adorable... I give up. One date, OK?

Her: Great, what are you doing Friday?

This girl was like a Mack truck coming through. I vaguely remember being described that way myself. When was that again?

We had four dates. The fifth one didn't count because she showed up an hour late, having gotten blotto with her soccer team. Sloppy drunk is acceptable for a 22-year-old, when she's partying with her gang of buddies, but it's no fun if you're over 30, conscious, and don't want to have a public make-out session with her—with, I might add, the rest of her soccer team watching. They were clearly impressed with my older-woman status, but I also suspect half of them had crushes on her and were secretly delighted when I untangled myself and left.

It wasn't until I had to write this book that I remembered my own youthful "What does age matter?" affair. And some people seem to always be attracted to someone 10 or 15 years older or younger. Does it matter? Guess that all depends on your vantage point.

Top 10 Things You Don't Want to Hear on a First Date

10. Any sentence that contains the phrase "restraining order."

9. "My girlfriend, I mean, ex-girlfriend—well, you know how it is—they're never really exes, are they?

8. "My therapist thinks it was really just too much Thorazine."

7. "Yep, got me a sweet one-bedroom—just me, my four dogs, six cats, and a goat."

6. "I don't know if I'm a top or bottom, butch or femme, so how about you tell me what you are and I'll be the other?"

5. "Evone? Oh, that's a nickname my first lover gave me and it stuck. What? Oh, it's short for 'Evil One.' "

4. "Hey, you want to go to my prom?"

3. "My ex-boyfriend just got out of jail, and he's not too crazy about me being with women now, but I changed my phone number and all."

2. "I'm not nearly as bulimic as I used to be, but that *was* a lot of pasta—I'll be right back."

1. "Excuse me, but I'm about to have a psychotic breakdown, so promise me you won't take it personally, OK? I said, *OK?!*"

Bi and Bi-Curious Girls and Dykes Who Occasionally Sleep With Men

This is, after all, the brave new world, the beginning of the new millennium, and as such we must embrace all the diversity our community keeps coming up with. Things are changing so quickly, one can barely keep up with the lingo, which is why the word *queer* is so damn handy. Especially for those who want that one word to cover pretty much anyone who isn't a missionary-position conservative heterosexual.

As of this writing, a new term just wafted my way through a friend. She's having her first affair with a man, which now makes her bisexual. She's debating whether that's the best term for her, since this affair could be a fluke and she really likes being a gay girl of the lesbian variety. I told her I think that the term *gay girl* can cover both, and after all, I am writing a book the subject, so I should know. My friend's new male lover is in an open marriage (with a woman and child and all those license and tax breaks), and he considers himself "heteroflexible." That's definitely one for semantics scholars and the queer lexicon. Oh, but this is San Francisco. God, I love this town.

Now, once and for all, I'd like to dispel the nasty rumor that bisexuals are more promiscuous than the average bear. Puh-leeze. I'll bet this rumor was started by some jealous, bitter, celibate person. After all, sexuality is all over the place, literally and figuratively. Even the Kinsey Report, so esteemed by the mainstream medical establishment, claims, "Men are more rigid and consistent in their sexual object choices; women are flexible and fluid." I swear that's a direct quote.

For years and years, lesbians have been suspicious of their bisexual sisters. Many won't even consider dating them, lest they, I don't know, see a cute guy and drop said lesbian like a "gay hot potato." I understand there is that part of the psyche that resents how the bisexual woman is accorded heterosexual "privilege" whenever she's dating a man, etc, etc. Not entirely accurate, according to some of my bisexual girlfriends. They feel like they don't fit anywhere, because lots of women won't date them, but they don't feel comfortable in the completely straight world either. They, too, have to negotiate—i.e., *Do I tell them now I'm queer? Does it matter? But if I don't, I'll feel like an imposter.* Same old, same old.

Though I would be remiss if I didn't relate one experience a friend of mine had with her nonmonogamous bisexual lover. Let's call the lover Cindy. After much persuading, my friend was talked into a friendly meal at her place, to meet Cindy's other lover, a man. At this point I can hear the screams: *Setup!* Which in fact it was. Now, call my friend naive, but at that point she was curious, having never been put in this kind of situation. Granted, by the time he not so subtly opened the third bottle of wine she should have called a cab, unless she was into it. By coffee and brandy, inhibitions neatly tucked out of the way, she and her lover got frisky. The guy mysteriously disappeared. It wasn't until my friend realized he had reappeared and really did want to watch that she got grossed out, put on her shirt inside out, and stormed out of the house. It would have been a great exit, but she desperately needed a cab, so she had to knock and ask them to call her one. Still, she had her pride, and she insisted on waiting outside—in Massachusetts…in January. In all fairness, my friend did know that something was up beforehand but went anyway. And no matter how hip, slick, and cool she tried to be about it, she realized she felt a deep resentment because Cindy and her boy lover had the approval of church and state. But when Cindy was with my friend and they wanted to hold hands, they had to stick to certain neighborhoods or risk being taunted or worse. It's safe to say that it was over with Cindy by the first morning's light.

Now, the category "dykes who sleep with men occasionally" is a tad puzzling to me. It would logically follow that these girls are bisexual, but no, they are still dykes. I suspect this might be a bit bi-phobic. This society is *so* into the binary system of either/or: There are only two choices, so you'd better step right up and pick. And no dillydallying about who *you* want to be or are—pick one and be done with it already! Who comes up with these arbitrary rules? I know, I know it's all about social controls, etc., but get over it. That's an order.

Which brings us to the category of bi-curious, or as I think of it, that first tentative peek out of the closet. There's nothing wrong with going slow, and there's always some gay girl who likes to be "the first" and is more than happy to help you explore. But if that first make-out session lasts through the weekend, the slide from bi-curious to bisexual is quick.

I used to joke that I was bisexual until I actually kissed a girl, whereupon I became a full-on card-carrying lesbian-dyke-gay girl. Anything that felt that good couldn't be wrong. No matter what the legal system, the culture, or my mother thought. But that's just me.

Recently, while I was writing this book, a former student of mine offered me carte blanche to assist me with all things Mac (I'm a G4 girl), as that's his day job. Let's call him Tom. I figured, hey, finally some fringe benefits for being a teacher. How many Mac specialists are going to love my Women in Film class so much they'll offer free computer service (going rate, $90 an hour). I should have been a little wary, but he seemed such a stand-up type guy, he could be one of my brothers. And he did give me his card twice and insist that I take him up on it. As I'm relatively ignorant of most things computer, beyond E-mail and, say, word processing, I called him a few months later and got some free and very useful lessons.

Then I decided to buy an iBook (laptop), which made sense, since I was writing a book and who can stand their own digs 24/7? Again, Tom fit me into his busy schedule to help me make a good selection. I neglected to add that Tom is very charming, over 30, and at some point I realized he was "testing the waters" by flirting with me. OK, I noticed during the first lesson, but I'm a playful sort and it never crossed the line into icky (that's the technical term). He knows I'm a gay girl, we laugh a lot, and he'd be a fun friend, so I figured I couldn't blame a guy for trying. I'd mentioned enough gay-girl-type stories and details to him that I knew he was clear on where I'd drawn the line in the sand, or libido, as the case might be.

But while taking him out to a thank-you dinner, I found out he had four ex-girlfriends who were strictly lesbians before dating him. I looked at him, laughed, and said, "Well, I'm not number five…" He laughed too. Then I thought, *Oh, my God, have I acquired my very own dyke-dude?* Dyke-dude: an expression that comic Mark Davis and I came up with years ago. (We never managed to make that skit work…hmm, maybe we could now.) Dyke-dude: cute, huh? That would be the gay-girl/straight-guy equivalent of the long-standing tradition of the gay guy with the straight woman best friend. Yes, I know the expression for the latter, but it's gone outside the tribe and now sounds derogatory. Or to be clearer, it's the role Rupert Everett is most likely to play opposite some straight woman megastar. Turns out Tom is even close friends with a fairly famous lesbian writer. Big surprise. And because Tom is what my parents would call a "gentleman" he never pushes or makes me uncomfortable, but continues to charm me. And I've been single for close to six months.

Jokingly, while I was complaining about coming up with more essays for this very book, he said, "Oh, just go out with me already, Mo—that's worth a chapter." We both laughed, and I couldn't decide if I was intrigued or really that desperate for another essay. It has been, oh, 15 years since I knew a man in the biblical sense. This is the new millennium, after all, and no one else nearly as good-looking and funny has asked me out in ages. Why don't they make the girl version of Tom?

Even months after that dinner, I'm still considering Tom's offer—which freaks me out. My friends are worried that celibacy is affecting my judgment. Actually, celibacy always affects my judgment, generally not in a good way—not in the long run, anyway. But it makes for great copy. I haven't completely ruled Tom out, though I somehow can't imagine a whole lot past the kissing part. Without getting too explicit, if you're going to date and eventually have sex with someone, you can't decide ahead of time that there are certain things you just are not going to do.

Still, we could have a date, I'd find out the kissing is bland, and that'd be the end of it. But if four gay girls before me went for it, odds are he's a pretty good kisser. And then there's the weirdness factor. After being with women so long, will I suddenly be repulsed or feel inept? My friend Karla once commented that I was the most lesbian gay girl she's ever met, a 100 percenter. I'd like to think I'm more like 95%. It's just that I haven't had my 5% seriously challenged in a long time. So far I'm hoping some luscious gay girl rescues me *fast*. I'm quickly sliding into to the "why not?" category on this. I mean, I don't have to do anything I don't want to do, and it would give me a few more insights for this chapter. What's a girl to do?

My fence sitting aside, I applaud all these different choices because, let's face it, sexual repression has lead to such noble endeavors as the Spanish Inquisition, miscegenation laws, and the Religious Right—not to mention the more bizarre manifestations of our consumer culture. I mean, if one was having scrumptious hot sex, would one *really* need to own a $50,000 car with vanity plates reading "BIG 1 4U." I think not. You'd be perfectly happy driving anything that brought you physically closer to the object of your affection. Need I say more?

OK, maybe I will. Now, I understand that for political reasons it's much more effective to have a united front, say that we're all "gay people," "queer," or the most inclusive/specific lesbian, gay, bisexual, transgender. One problem with the latter, though, is that there are those transsexual people who fall under the transgender umbrella who are dating the other sex and who consider themselves heterosexual and therefore not queer at all. Of course, there are many transsexual people who do identify with the queer nation.

My point is that including every individual choice to identify the community can be cumbersome and politically confusing. In a culture as obsessed and terrified of sex as the U.S., it's a very tricky political card to play to begin with. But play it we must, or we'll be censored out of existence and driven back to the shame and hiding of years past.

None of this should stop anyone from expressing their true selves, experimenting, or in general having safe, fun sex. Now, that was a very long stretch of me not being funny. Our president, Mr. Shrub—no Einstein, he—occupies the highest office in the land and forces me into such fits of reality that no matter which way I squeeze, transmute, or modify, this part comes out serious. I would apologize, but I think I get one comic lapse per book per my contract. So, I say enjoy to all the hyphenated, polysyllabic fusions of new and specific sexual identities. Me? In general, I don't think I have the energy or predilection for being anything other than a "one gay girl at a time" type. But I love knowing I *could be* if the urge kicked in.

The Internet or Great Love Highway

The Internet—that great pool of information and endless possibilities, the Great Love Highway. I-dating is now so commonplace that I suspect that's why every single woman has a Palm Pilot. You can flirt 24/7, then wander off the landscape without apologizing, processing, or in any other way being accountable. This is not entirely a bad thing.

First, a word of caution if you haven't actually tried I-dating: Beyond cigarettes, crack, or Froot Loops, I-dating is definitely addictive—at least during that first week.

It works like this. First, you put up your "profile," a term previously reserved for the FBI or your face positioned at a 180-degree angle. Profiles vary from Web site to Web site, but basically you provide your stats and what you're looking for in a woman. What does this mean? *Sell, sell, sell, sell.* Tell your future Ms. Right exactly who you are and why she can't live without you.

Within a few surfing sessions, you'll quickly realize there are those who surf and pick but do not have profiles and those who have profiles and sit back and wait for the mail. Then there are those women who play it both ways in order to maximize their odds. I, of course, being an impatient sort and given to the immersion method, played it both ways.

The first time you create your profile, you may be delighted to see that you have received three whole letters.

(I still think of E-mail that way. I mean they are letters, aren't they? It's just that one doesn't have to keep up with the new postal rates and actually *walk* to a mailbox. I'm convinced that with the Internet and 550 cable stations we soon won't have to ever go into the outdoors at all. The outdoors—that's where they keep the weather, for those of you already hooked up.)

Anyway, that first time you see that strangers have found you interesting and have taken the time to send you E-mails, well, it's like *so* flattering. Then you read them.

There might be one pretty good response—someone you might actually be able to have a conversation with. She'll have actually read your profile in detail and written back specifics that pique your curiosity. Then there'll be one that clearly was written very late at night after an overly festive evening; it won't be without charm, but it won't quite make sense either. And then there'll be one that says, "Liked your profile. If you like mine, call me @ 555-6969." This one will scare you, as it should. How can someone just give out her phone number like that? You could be a seriously deranged, needy, actually heterosexual, and "looking for a place to crash" sort of person. You're not, but you *could* be.

Do you know that conversations used to be considered so personal they had things called phone booths? I've seen them in movies, and people actually stepped inside to make a call so that (a) strangers would not overhear your personal business and (b) strangers would not be burdened with overhearing your personal business. I personally think people talking on cell phones in public should have a little plastic silencing dome they attach to their face that prevents the casual pedestrian from being burdened in this way. I *so* do not want to hear about your dental extraction—in detail.

Back to the Internet profiles: All those questions you have to answer, all those moral decisions such as: Am I truly like this or is this what I would *like* to be like? Do I leave out that I eat pretzels compulsively when I'm nervous, or is that a "telling" detail? Am I revealing too much? If I don't identify as a top or bottom, as butch or femme, will women think I have no sex life or that I'm wishy-washy?

Then the whole picture/no picture question. If I insist on receiving one, am I being "lookist"? After all, chemistry isn't entirely based on visuals. I always include a photo with my profile so prospective dates will get to see what I look like. OK, my picture *is* very blurry—I'm not sure why it turned out that way, but one can glean the basic idea.

Why, when scanning the profiles and I come across someone's picture that tells me I don't think they're "my type," do I feel guilty and read their profile anyway—knowing that it's very unlikely that I'll write to this person? It seems very cruel to pass over a woman simply because she's not photogenic or "cute enough"—in whatever way one thinks of as "cute." Knowing that I'm also one of those passed-over people makes the whole thing *so* tricky. There's a hint of "Dating Darwinism" here, but I can't quite put my finger on it.

As an experiment, I decided to meet three very different women via the Internet—unless of course I fell madly in love with #1 or #2, then all bets would be off. Though my cynic within was dubious, my optimistic romantic was intrigued.

Meet #1

The entire experience is flattering: *She* found me, wrote poetic and witty letters, and called me first. Since, personality-wise, I'm on the extreme end of "not shy," I'm always delighted when someone pursues me. Being an I-date virgin, however, I have to say the I-dating thing initially intimidated me.

We decide on meeting in a fancy gay restaurant lounge for a casual drink. I pick her up at where she works, once she's off for the day—on my motor scooter, no less. I am nothing if not glamorous. Most working artists are, you know. This is after all, only a "meet." You don't want to commit to more time than it takes to down a Coke, in case it's a total "Oh, my God, get me outta here" situation.

She's surprisingly pretty and has a great smile, definitely femme all the way. Let's call her Ingrid. She's just as charming as her letters: quirky and funny, endlessly easy to chat with. I decide there must be something wrong with her. Perhaps she has one of these "meets" every weekend, goes home and tells her not-quite ex-roomie about them, and they laugh through the night. OK, I'm a tad paranoid, but I've had some very odd dates in my life too.

The evening goes swimmingly. We're both flirting our asses off and generally enjoying each other. The "meet" ends more like a "date" with a rather long good-night kiss. I am liking this I-dating thing.

We have two more dates. On date three she tells me she isn't actually sure if she's still a lesbian. She was until a couple months ago, she explains, until she dated this guy. Then she stops talking. I wait. Finally, trying to suss out exactly what she's trying to tell me, I ask her point-blank.

Me: So, are you bisexual?
Ingrid: I don't know… He's the first man I've ever dated.
Another lengthy pause.
Me: Wait—are you still dating him?
Ingrid: I don't know.
Me: You mean you can't *tell*?
Ingrid: No, I —
I volunteer the "it's over" axe.
Me: Tell you what: It doesn't sound like it's a good idea for us to date—especially if you can't *tell* if you're actually dating this man and have no idea if you're still a lesbian or what…ever. It's OK. These things happen.

But internally I'm thinking, *Not to me or anyone I know.* Especially that part about not being sure if you're still dating someone or not. Especially in light of the fact that *you* wooed me on the Net, not the other way around.

She concedes that I'm right, but she *really* likes me, or so she tells me as she walks me to my scooter. I smile, put on my helmet, and ride into the well-lit San Francisco night.

When I check my E-mail the next day, there's a long and charming letter from Ingrid, as though nothing has happened. It's the same flirtatious tone, the adorable and original quirky writing style. Was I the only one present during that bizarre conversation? Huh?

I write a brief but firm note, saying that not dating anymore includes not writing to each other. I know bisexuality can hit anytime and that's fine. But pursuing another woman when you're still sort of not sure if you are in fact still dating a man? That's out of my league. I'm way too tired to figure out where I would fit or even want to fit into that configuration, particularly only two dates into it.

So I go back to the Net, still determined to have "meets" with three different women. And I mean *different.* Ingrid was very femme, so I want the next girl to be butch. And I find her.

Meet #2

She's very cute, not exactly handsome, but plenty butch—in her photo anyway. We agree to a very chaste "meet" at a café that I suggest and set it for 11 A.M. the following Sunday (good-night kisses are less likely in broad daylight). I don't go to this particular café on Sundays very often; it's packed with families, and toddlers and infants abound.

I get there 15 minutes early to stake out a good seat. Good thing too. I get lucky: A pack of mommies and kids spread over three tables are leaving. I pick a table next to the wall to give us some sense of privacy or at least not being in the fray. The spot is also out of any direct sunlight, so the appallingly large red PMS pimple that appeared on the tip of my nose this very morning will look, I hope, less frightening.

I order a double latte. PMS makes self-destructive behavior so much more enjoyable. The constant sing-song repetition of "Mommy, mommy, where's my juice?" is working my very last PMS nerve. My pimple has probably tripled in size since I last looked, and I wonder if there's a graceful way to work into a conversation that I usually have pretty decent skin and today's blemish is just a demonic manifestation of my estrogen level.

She arrives. Very cute and very butch, she is. Let's call her Lee. We exchange a "Wow, I didn't think you'd be like this" type of look. We are both dressed down, clearly in anticipation of a nonmatch. The pheromones are flowing as freely as the espresso. The conversation is easy, so after lattes she asks if I'd like to see a movie sometime. "Sure," I say. I wonder whether I should ask if she's dated any men lately, but I refrain, as she did say her last relationship ended more than a year ago and, well, she's way too butch to date a guy. Actually, she admits, that until she starts talking she gets mistaken for a man all the time.

In the coming week, Lee and I write and chat a few times, then go out on a date. At evening's end there's another rather prolonged good-night kiss. After say, 10 minutes or so, she suddenly she realizes she isn't quite over her ex and is uncomfortable. She is truly sorry and keeps apologizing. "It's fine," I say. "Really." She writes me the following day to apologize again. I like her and am sorry that timing is everything, and we clearly don't have timing.

I'm two for two. I'm beginning to wonder if I'm the girl most likely to be chosen to figure out if you're still into/not over your ex. Like a divining rod to water, only I point you in the direction of your true love, and it's away from me. They say three's the charm, which I am seriously doubting at this point, even though two of my friends have met and are actively in love with their dream girl, whom they met through the Great Internet Love Highway. Both friends were actually inspired by my own forays in the world of I-dating. Well, someone should be happy.

I think the oddest thing about I-dating is that you don't get to see how the woman is "in the world." By that I mean, it seems that mostly we end up dating people we know through work, school, friends, sports, or various group activities. These situations give us plenty of chances to see how the object of our budding affection interacts with the world, other people, etc. With I-dating, we only know what they tell us and what we can glean from a few short meetings. How can you trust someone who might end up being a great writer of fiction? (And I don't mean novels.) How can you trust your pheromones and a few E-mails with your delicate feelings, etc? I'm more paranoid than most, having been a comic who naively dated two different women who got seriously turned on watching me perform. Both asked me to repeat a "bit" I did as a kind of foreplay. Needless to say, it freaked me out and made me more suspicious of people. Therefore, I don't take people at their word, firmly believing that actions speak louder than words.

Another thing: I-dating is a lot of work. All that letter writing, trying to weed out the "No, we wouldn't get alongs" from the "She is *so* charmings." Then there's the "Who offers a phone number first?" dynamic. I'm pretty timid about that, even though the three or four people I eventually talked to seemed to be normal nonstalker types. That said, onto the next I-date.

Meet #3

This one actually never took place. I wrote to her first, she wrote back enthusiastically, and two letters later (or one volley) she asked if I wanted to meet for tea or dinner—how was this Saturday for me? I wrote back a couple of time options, gave her my phone number, and said we should probably talk first. Saturday came and went, and she never called or wrote. I thought that was pretty rude, barring, say, her being in a major car accident and having to wear a full-body cast.

A few days later this was still bugging me, so I wrote a short, very innocuous, nonaccusatory "What happened?" type note. A few days after that, she wrote back, and I quote:

> sorry about…(really, dot-dot-dot) but I guess this
> whole blind-date/internet thing wigs me out, so I
> sort of just floated off…

That was it. No name to or from, not even the traditional capital initial, no hello or goodbye, just this ambiguous "sorry, dot-dot-dot": *About WHAT?* Say it—you flaked! You asked to meet me and then just *blew me off*!

Do I sound bitter?

What boggles my mind is that she, obviously a sensitive sort, didn't realize that there was an actual real live person with her own delicate feelings on the other end of these notes. Someone she liked well enough to take the initiative and be the first one to suggest a meet. I don't get it.

Oh, and I checked: She still had her profile up a week later. Why? So she could correspond with someone who'd get excited about the romantic possibilities, then blow that person off because she's not into blind dating? I mean how long does it take to write, "Sorry, this weekend won't work," or "I apologize, but I don't think I'm up to this I-dating thing"? Come on, if you've never run across each other in real life all this time, it's unlikely you will anytime soon. Why be rude or self-conscious? No one is so busy that they don't have two minutes to do the right thing.

So that's my final statement about I-dating. It is now written in *Mo Brownsey's Rules of Life and Love* (to be published after this book, though much shorter—it's more like a pamphlet):

> Thou shalt not treat an I-date person with any less respect than you would anyone else. Just because she's not tangible or in the room, a known in-the-flesh reality, doesn't mean she's not a person who, like yourself, is taking that same risk by posting a personals ad.

And that is all she wrote.

Long-distance Dating or LDD

We've all done long-distance dating (LDD), and when the romance ends, we curse ourselves nine times out of 10 when that last phone bill comes in. What could we have been talking about all that time? My most memorable post-breakup phone bill was more than $500 from an affair I had with a woman in Montreal (or as I like to refer to it, *"Je t'aime,* my ass."). Granted, I was on the road most of that summer and using a calling card with great abandon. I was truly a fool for love and the convenience of that little plastic number-dense card.

I was a touring comic for four years (1992-1996), so I was more susceptible to LDDs than your average bear. My technique at one point was to keep all my women in different time zones. It sharpened my math skills—all that adding and subtracting one, two, or three hours—and gave me a greater appreciation of how vast this country truly is. Thank God I never dated anyone from Germany; I can *never* figure out what time it is there.

The trick to LDD is figuring out whether the relationship is based on more than just great sexual chemistry. The planned visits are usually weeks or even months apart—depending on airfares, how long the long distance is, your income and hormone levels, and the limit on your credit cards. By the time you get to see each other, you spend all your time in bed until, weak with hunger, you creep out into the world in search of sustenance. And I must add, no matter how hard you try, everyone at the store, restaurant, or Taco Bell will take one look at your dazed-out bliss and know that you two are among the very sexually satiated. And they will hate you for it. It could be homophobia, but it's just as likely to be jealousy.

How do you know it's not just lust? Do you care? "Just lust" is nothing to sneeze at. It's good for your libido, psyche, and can provide months of fun. But at some point, between the money, travel hassles, organizing pet care, house-sitters, and one person leaving her life for a three- to four-day stretch, it's either going to move past lust or die.

I must also mention that if you live in San Francisco, New York City, or Los Angeles, and your new love lives in small-town kill-the-homos USA, you will probably be the host more often. This is a big advantage, but don't rub it in. She too will enjoy being in a place where she can safely hold your hand in public, but she'll also be missing her dogs, pillows, and being able to find the bathroom in the dark.

Unimpeded by personality differences, great sex can only last so long. Eventually she will admit to something you hadn't expected, like voting for George Bush. That happened to me, and I swear the kissing was suddenly not quite right after that. And as we all know, when the kissing goes, it's a fast slide downhill to unexciting sex. Dull sex does not merit $500 phone bills or $400 plane rides—unless you're independently wealthy and having affairs outside your time zone is a hobby. In which case, look me up; I'm generally borderline broke and love to travel.

How do you get to know someone in her daily life if you're never there for it? In the Internet age, E-mail and instant messaging can help you get to know someone in an interesting way. Though, as I discussed in the last essay on I-Dating, the charming, witty, ethical, compassionate E-mail lover could turn out to be the petty, controlling, obsessive-compulsive sort after that third in-person visit. So with E-mail, as with most of life, you have to read between the lines.

Then there's the old-fashioned way: the phone. This is by far the most utilized tool for the LDD. If you're smart, you'll accept one of the introductory phone-war offers at the start of the LDD. They generally will give you $50 worth of free minutes and a low introductory rate. And by the time you've used up the free minutes, your old phone company should be wooing you back with another $50 certificate. Take it. The airlines will give you nothing but frequent flyer miles, and I assure you you'll need them.

Of course, you might actually end up falling in love with your LDD lover. If this happens, eventually someone must move. This situation I know firsthand.

As I mentioned earlier, great sexual chemistry in a LDD liaison goes a long way toward rationalizing the hassles, expense, and time spent away from home. But what happens if you and your little crumpet d'amour move beyond the sex into the feelings and falling-in-L— department?

It's especially tough for me, since I'm not one to jump on the L— bandwagon with abandon. No second-date U-Haul for this gay girl. I learned my lesson from a previous LDD. I met someone (I'll call her Woman A) on the road, but being on the road, a month or so later I met Woman B. I slept with B—had sex in the legal sense (or illegal, depending on the state). Since there were immediate feelings, I had to tell Woman A; hence, her cursing my name as loud as the day is long—or at least crying for $200 worth of time on my phone card. It was the least I could do, and I still feel bad about that one.

Things got serious with Woman B. I had enough relative youth, stamina, and whatever romantic/psychic/delusional state that I fell in love with her before the end of the week. Two months later, I helped her pack up her things on the East Coast, and together we drove the 3,000 miles back to San Francisco, where she moved into my flat.

I have to point out that both affairs happened under the auspices of my being the lezzie comic in town. Lesbians love comedy (see Ellen DeGeneres) and, as an extension, love comics just as much. It's sort of like how gay men love their porn stars; lesbians love the women who make them laugh. Which explains why one popular but mean-spirited and plain-looking comic *always* has a flawless beauty on her arm.

Is this whole comic-allure thing looking clearer, or do I just sound like a sex-crazed lesbian lounge lizard riding that "Haven't I seen you before—and did I mention I'm a comic?" wave, replete with sparkly tux jacket, slicked-back hair, dangling cigarette, and a generally suave yet slimy way about me?

Falling in L— (OK, *Love*—you can see how phobic I am) when you're in an LDD can be so damn tricky. Especially when you've been on both sides of the broken-heart scenario.

Unless you meet and stay with your lover when you're in your 20s, by your mid 30s you get as cautious as a Republican trying to woo the ACLU. How do you know if she's only wearing her Sunday-best personality for you on those short visits after you've spent weeks apart? Or at the other end of the spectrum, a major bone of contention comes up and you have a fight on the phone. By the time you've "processed" it, you've sent half of MCI's employees' children through college (or least to summer camp).

So when do you know that the LDD is worth your committing to saying to people "My lover, who lives in XYZ...?" I've developed a new approach and theory. Wait until you've made it through three major holidays before you make it official. A few years ago, I started an LDD in June, so Independence Day counted (but not Labor Day or any other Monday holiday, especially Columbus Day, which in San Francisco is celebrated as Indigenous Peoples Day). Because we're queer, Halloween, *the* gay high holiday, counts (a friend aware of my holiday rule said Halloween should count for two). We got through Thanksgiving, so then it was official and I started referring to her as my girlfriend. Oh, and at that point the L-word was being used freely between the two of us. It was pure heaven.

part three

Sex

- how to tell lust from love
- the mystery of pheromones explored
- the depths of the soul—or something more anatomical—on fire
- sex legislated, a sad tale indeed

The Power of Sex

Ah, sex, that moment of perfection, when there's nothing but glorious sensation, no words, no separation. It's like your molecules blend with everything—your lover, the sheets (or rubber mat, as the case may be). For this moment and all that leads up to it, most people are willing, at one time or another, to risk everything. And I mean everything: See Bill Clinton. That man risked (and lost) being one of the greatest statesmen—certainly one of the smartest—in living memory. But no, the possibility of that moment was so compelling that he went for it (or her).

When people marveled at his stupidity, all I could think was, yeah, pretty dumb in terms of choice, but people have always risked their very lives, livelihoods, families—the whole ball of wax (or lube)—for sex. Queer people especially know this. Sex is stronger than any of our other instincts, except for breathing, and we only have that so we can have more sex. Really, I read it somewhere. And even if I didn't, you know it's true.

Earlier in human evolution, sex was simply a fun thing you did with whoever was handy. Sometime after, oh, 5,000 or 10,000 years, those first Homo sapiens (see, we *are* everywhere) connected the "wild thing" with childbirth. Fast-forward, say, oh, umm, 50,000 years (think of this as very ballpark Mo-science) and sex is connected to romance, marriage, lineage, state, church, and numerous television shows. At least that was the idea. Though all of us know, straight or gay, that it's perfectly possible and potentially very enjoyable to have sex with someone we barely know, rather than are bound to till death do you part.

Take the insect kingdom: As many of you might know, the female black widow eats her male mate after copulating with him. Now, you'd think that at some point these guys would catch on: "Hey, where's Larry? Last I saw him, he was on his way to Linda's." But no, they keep lining up for that (literal) *petite morte* (French for "little death," which is slang for male orgasm).

Look at the history of queer culture and queer-identified lives. For most of modern history, say from the 16th century on, to act on same-sex desire could cost you your life, home, family, and job. Unfortunately, this is probably still true for many people all across this and other countries.

Sure, Plato and his buddies had it easy, devising an entire culture on the ideal love being between two men—one young, pre-beard, who is mentored by an older man (with full beard…say between 30 and 70 years old. OK, maybe not 70, but 50 was acceptable). Sure, there were strict rules about when and how any affection or sexual activity took place. It was primarily about teaching the boy how to be a thinker, a good citizen, a sophisticated person. But male-male coupling was also considered the highest, purest type of love. They even theorized that an army of lovers fighting side by side could rule the world. Of course, this embracing of same-sex love didn't include women. In fairness, Plato's *Symposium* does offer one mention of lesbian existence. And yes, that is the word used, *lesbian*—Sappho and her lot living in relatively the same time period. In general, however, in Plato's republic, women were seen as a necessary evil. Heterosexuality was acted on in weaker moments, and it did have the benefit of keeping Athens populated. Therefore, queerness has not always been seen as an "alternative lifestyle" or worse, "a manifestation of Satan."

In short, heterosexual marriage as the only acceptable expression of adult love is a relatively new idea in the scheme of things and not for everyone. Therefore it begs the philosophical question: Is doing the wild thing on a first date sleazy, normal/healthy, a sign of intimacy issues, or a great way to kill a rainy afternoon? Personally, I think it's all or any of the above, depending on the person, situation, and the agreement going in. That, of course, is the rub: communication. When it comes to sex, we are all either frighteningly monosyllabic or overly chatty. While one person is delighted by this chance but more than likely short-lived encounter (for some that means hours), it is for the other person the start of a beautiful romance. This is where most country-western music comes from (a non sequitur, I know, but there's only so long one can write specifically about sex without a break).

Why is sex so compelling? I leave it to persons more poetic than me. I do know that I once had an eight-month affair with a (single) woman with whom I could barely hold a conversation. We totally brought out the worst in each other's personalities, but our sex was on fire. We're talking all-weekend-long sex marathons—as long as we didn't talk too much. Especially pre-sex. Post-sex, for some reason, we got along much better. I once told her I thought it a good idea that I meet her at the door in a state of undress so that we wouldn't talk too long before the big event—the only event, really, for us anyway. And of course it got messy and nasty at the end. Being gay girls, we lacked the gay-male gene for perspective on these things.

As with all pleasurable things, pain seems to march in tandem with sex. You pay and pay and pay, at least in my experience. It's a rare gay-girl coupling that has ongoing intimate relations without an almost equal amount (eventually) of discussion, working on the issues/compromises, etc. Why is the universe so harsh in this way? Why can't some things be left unexplained, untarnished, *unprocessed*?

In many places in the world, including in this country, being a gay girl can be fraught with all kinds of risk. Yet here we are, gay girls reading an up-front book about queer romance and sex—and all the dilemmas thereof—and mainstream bookstores are willing to sell us copies. Obviously, some women will choose discretion on a bus in small-town Georgia (or Texas or New York...upstate). But thankfully, some won't.

The Dreaded Lesbian Bed Death

Solution:

SEX=LOVERS

NO SEX = FRIENDS

REPEAT

SEX = LOVERS

NO SEX = FRIENDS

Repeat anytime you get confused.

Vibrating Down South

A few years ago, my friend Jody, born and raised in Birmingham, Alabama, shared a bizarre news clipping from *The San Francisco Chronicle* with me. It was so weird I kept it. In April 1999 (the year is worth repeating, you'll see), the Alabama state legislature ruled that if you want to buy a vibrator you'd have to cross state lines. The law reads, in part, that the sale or purchase of "any device designed or marketed as useful primarily for the stimulation of human genitals" is prohibited in the state of Alabama.

Let's say that men hold 90% of Alabama's senate seats. That far south of the Mason-Dixon Line, 90% is a conservative figure. Anyway, the point is that this overwhelmingly straight male group of senators actually discussed and voted to ban the sale of vibrators in their state. The legal reason given: Women do not have a constitutional right to orgasm. Come again? Apparently not in Alabama.

The obvious question is, who wrote this bill and why? Was some poor senator being harassed daily by those pesky door-to-door vibrator salespeople? Were the vibrator catalogs just stacking up in the vestibule? Was the bill's author annoyed by all the vibrator kiosks lining the city streets, when all he wanted was a corn dog—the edible kind?

These same senators, it should be noted, said nary a word when Viagra came on the market. I'm sure their reasoning had something to do with Bob Dole, medical efficacy, and propagation of the species. It would seem there's no need for discussion concerning a man's constitutional right to orgasm. My strong suspicion? Straight men don't want anyone to have fun without them.

Not all straight men feel this way—just enough of them in Alabama's senate to pass such a ridiculous law. What's next, banning the sale of vibrating beds ("like a million little fingers" a quarter at a time), those BarcaLounger massage chairs, and motorcycles (but only for women)? I myself have a vibrating hairbrush that massages your scalp as you brush your hair. Could I carry that across state lines?

I'm trying very hard to restrain myself from making fun of a state whose reputation for sophistication falls somewhere between liking beef jerky and family gatherings to watch *World's Worst Car Crashes Caught Live On Video.* But to quote my friend Jody, "There are lots of sweet things about Alabama, forward thinking not being one of them."

How does a woman's right to orgasm become a constitutional question *at all*? Granted, we are talking about the state senate that, in that same session, was putting up a fight over the repeal of the archaic law that bans interracial marriages. I'm not making this up. Need I say more?

Well, actually, I do. Conveniently, the anti-repeal folks argument was that a repeal of this law would leave the door wide open for same-sex marriages. If vibrators freak these guys out, I can only imagine their enlightened stance on Stan and Larry getting hitched at city hall. This is all true. Look it up on the Internet.

Sex and control: Not too hard to see how their interplay might affect queers and especially women, so it's like a double whammy for gay girls and a triple whammy for gay girls of color. Did someone shake the country so that all the white heterosexual males with serious control issues around sex ended up as Alabama state senators? I photocopied that clipping before it got too ratty to read so I could remind myself that we might be everywhere, but so are they. And some of them are not very happy.

Since then, a higher court struck down the vibrator ban. But the fact that it passed at all in Alabama's senate, a group comprised of educated, elected officials, is very troubling. Are they scared that if the women folk can self-pleasure via vibrator, they'll either hightail it to a more liberal state or maybe (gasp) become *lesbians*? It's fairly well-known that at one time or another 99% of all lesbians have purchased or used a vibrator. There is at least an unconscious connection between the lesbian and the vibrator, even in Alabama. Therefore, I will go out on a very skinny branch and hypothesize that the specter of lesbian "perversion" helped pass that bill in Alabama's senate. I don't have scientific proof—it's just my gut...opinion.

So, to all you gay girls down south, I say, stay strong, stay satiated, and if that doesn't work, move to a gay-friendlier state—of mind or geography, whichever comes first.

Chemistry: Where Does It Come From, Where Does It Go?

Ah, sexual chemistry, the great mystery of life, otherwise known as pheromones. Webster's dictionary lists but one definition for *pheromone:* "noun: any of a class of hormonal substances secreted by an individual and stimulating a physiological or behavioral response from an individual of the same species." The prefix *pher* comes from the Greek, meaning "to bear." To bear mones? I rather like the sound of "to bear moans." Kind of sexy, no? The definition includes the word *individual,* then distances pheromones from people by including the term *species.* When was the last time you heard someone speak of a zebra as an individual, as in "That individual was just eviscerated by a lion"? Granted, I'm sure animals of all sorts also have pheromones. But it does look like Webster's doesn't want to completely admit that actual people *also* secrete pheromones.

The fact that Webster's offers only one definition gives me the heads up that no one has even attempted to use this word for a second or third meaning, which is extremely unusual in the (American) English language. No one's messing with this word, not even to make it an adjective, adverb, or verb (except me). Look up the word *drag* and you'll see what I mean. There are 33 definitions, and to show you how low on the scale queer stuff is, we clock in at #27, with by far the shortest definition—slang: transvestite attire. WRONG. And we don't even get a sentence as an example like some of the other meanings. But we do get this nod before #28: "masonry, a steel plate with a serrated edge for dressing a stone surface." Webster also thinks definition #19 is used more commonly than #27: "a four-horse sporting and passenger coach with seats inside or on top." Gee, thanks. Words are so gosh-darn telling of a culture's dominant value systems and all that.

I find it very interesting that these mysterious phero-mones, usually based on smell, are connected to *species* sur-vival: sex or fear. Which would explain some of the more tragic romances I've participated in. What I perceived as incredible sexual chemistry was actually *fear,* my body telling me: "Mo: Run, run! Warp speed, sister! She's gonna chew you up, spit you out, then be pissed that you stained her carpet. RUN!" How can you tell the difference? Umm... Most of the time you can't, not right off. Which is, as one gets into her 30s, another good reason not to sleep with someone on the first date—even if your pheromones are screaming so loud you're pretty sure woodland creatures can hear them. But either resist or enter at your own peril.

Now, in my experience, the fear pheromone perceived as sexual chemistry has only happened three, maybe four times. Only one of these encounters lasted more than a month. (That's if you don't count the "I'll never sleep with a woman again—I'm buying a twin bed and throwing away all the toys" time of healing, which usually adds several months, but at least you're not being tortured from an outside source.) Only the first fear-or-sex lover lasted longer—four months—but by then she'd been so hideous, no amount of great make-up sex could be worth it, and I saw the pheromone for what it was: survival.

Now, another fun factoid is that pheromones are actually scents one gives off, not actual smells one can identify, like fresh baked bread. Pheromones work on a subconscious level. Close proximity can trigger their release. So basically, you are drawn to a person's scent, whether consciously or unconsciously. I have to admit that, looking back on most of the women with whom I've had the best chemistry, I did in fact like the way they smelled. Whether it was the soap they used, pheromones, perfume, or cologne, it attracted me. I actually forbade one of my lovers to wear her (men's) cologne because it overpowered her own scent and turned me off so badly. My request hurt her feelings, but I couldn't stand the smell of that Ralph Lauren stuff. There was no way I could feel amorous with it lingering in the air.

The question most of us get stuck on from time to time is, "Why don't I have chemistry with her?" I'm sure you've been there. For me, it goes something like this: She's perfect for me. We're both basketball nuts, love Jeanette Winterson, and make each other laugh; she's more than average-cute, *and* she's interested in me. So we go out, and I'm optimistic that I *will* become attracted to her in that special-woman way. I'm begging my stomach to do its squirrelly attraction thing, but nada. Nothing. We even try kissing, and it's fine— just not "I want to rip her clothes off" fine. *Why?* This isn't fair. Then I convince myself that maybe it'll grow in that direction. Maybe this is just what it feels like to be with someone who's actually good for me. Maybe, when you get older, it isn't the same crazed "I can't breathe, this is so good" feeling. Maybe mellow is better—a sign of maturity. Maybe…maybe it's just not going to happen.

So I'm back where I started. Chemistry is, unfortunately, totally arbitrary. But it seems like I'm becoming attracted to better and better people. It's almost like my pheromones are tired of the long breaks I have to take after an "all pheromones but nothing in common" affair. I'm still convinced you can have it all with the right gay girl. Of course, that doesn't mean it'll last forever, but the good part will be just as good as all those love songs claim (and without all the bad metaphors).

How to Tell Lust From Love: A Rambling Meditation

One of the most complicated aspects of having a new lover is the whole lust-versus-love thing. It's not exactly a competition, but the two can mimic each other and wreak havoc on your usually keen perception. This is especially true during those first weeks of gay-girl love, when each kiss is a mini-miracle, an explosion of delight and wonder. Truthfully, I still feel that way, but over the years I've become better at reading my pheromones and noticing actual personality traits—the real ones.

Lust can obscure all kinds of things: Someone's entire personality can disappear in a blink of desire fulfilled. You see, what happens is one generally superimposes the personality they want the person to have through what I call Sexually Transmitted Denial or STD. One or both persons can participate.

The problem here is that once you've started you must stick to your metaphoric guns. Whatever personality traits you have grafted onto your abject object of 24-hour sex marathons must not waver—not for a second. In actuality she may be a shy, quiet sort, but you wanted a witty, quirky sort, so no matter what she says, you must translate it to her STD personality. For example, she asks, "Have you seen my keys?" But you hear: "If I lose my keys one more time, I swear I'm going to pin them to my shirt like a third grader with a note: 'If lost return to...'" OK, not overly witty, but you have to make these things up fast before you notice the reality lag.

Sustaining a state of STD requires constant vigilance, and you can't let your conscious mind acknowledge it. Those with exceptional powers of denial fare quite well here; those of us who've been in therapy for a year or 10 may not do as well. For the latter, you may be able to hold on for, say, a month, six weeks on the outside.

But over time you will see little telltale signs: For instance, let's say you love movies—all movies—and she tells you she doesn't go to the movies anymore because with 900 cable stations why bother? And she already told you that the first time, anyway. *The first time?* you think. When was that? Oh, my God, I've got STD! What else have I missed? What?! You love Bruce Willis movies? And now I have to kiss you? How can I kiss a woman who loves all things Bruce Willis?

If you don't identify it, STD could last up to 10 years. And who says ignorance isn't bliss? (As long as you're still having killer sex, that is.) Though I do not recommend this, as you will still be essentially living with a sexy figment of your imagination.

Now, what happens if both people are in STD but one is in STD lust and the other in STD love? This is really tricky. Power imbalances are hell in all things romantic and especially complicated when STD is in play. Having been on both sides of this equation, as well as having walked many of my friends through the various permutations thereof, here are some handy tips.

STD Lust

If you're in lust but know this is not going to turn into love for you, and you're beginning to suspect that your lover is moving in the L-O-V-E direction, STD becomes crucial—that is, if you want to keep the affair going a while longer. Because no one wants to intentionally hurt anyone (well, most people), you have to be sure to "miss" any encroaching sign of deep feeling—for example, her arriving for a date with 12 exquisite long-stemmed red roses. Your STD would have to convince you that the roses are merely a very sweet manifestation of the lust you both share. Your gifts, though, run more to the sex toys/Victoria's Secret end of the spectrum but, all things being equal, are just as much tokens of your mutual lust. Both gifts fall into the no-strings lusty-affair category.

Sexually Transmitted Denial has an especially hard time continuing if she starts to say things like "So where do you see this going, you and me?" "To the nearest piece of furniture" is not the correct response. It is generally at this juncture that your lust STD will start to crumble and you'll only have two options: (1) Tell *a* truth—you really like her but need to play "this" by ear; or (2) tell her *the* truth—you like her but see "this" remaining in the dating/affair area. Because most people will want to save face, she will most likely say that she sees some possibility for something beyond dating but isn't totally sure what that might mean—or something to that effect. On the extreme end, she will tell you she's falling in love with you. If this happens, there will probably be what is called a "pregnant pause" (and for good reason—these situations can be as painful or joyful as child-birth).

Depending on whether any shred of STD remains as well as your level of maturity and compassion, this is one of those times when the kindest thing to do is to hurt someone's feelings. You will hurt them, and that is hard. This is in fact someone you are fond of—just not in love with. Leading someone on in this situation is not about your "sparing" their feelings; it's about sparing your own. So get out of your self-centered libido and do the right thing. Sure, you'll feel like a jerk and wish, oh wish, it were different for you. But it isn't. Carrying on this affair, while this perfectly nice sexy woman is looking for signs of your love, is mean. Sorry, there's no nice way to put it. She may hate you initially—but not as much as she will six months from now if you dodge and bob your way into prolonging the affair.

In rare cases, the in-love person will take you on your terms even though you know she's in love with you and you will never be. This is a truly difficult situation. You can try to go on for a few more months and see if your lust/fondness will grow into love. But if it doesn't (which is true more often than not), I offer the same advice: Do the right thing and get out.

STD Love

On the other end, let's say you're starting to have deeper and deeper feelings for your date/lover. You definitely have great sex, and the conversations seem to be getting better as time goes on. But why do you increasingly get this... umm...hesitation around her? That feeling that you can't entirely be yourself because you don't want her to know *how* much you like her. You'll start to compulsively analyze the simplest things: She asked what I was doing on Friday on a Wednesday—is that a good or bad sign? Does that mean she assumes we have a standing date as if we are a couple or that she takes me for granted? Should I have jumped in earlier and asked her out on Tuesday? Maybe she thinks I'm not that interested. I am, I *am* interested. Why can't I tell her? Will I scare her and put a premature end to all this great sex?

Eventually, all the interpretations of signs, conversations, and timetables will start to seriously chip away at your STD love. No matter which way you turn, you're going to start to feeling rejected. And that sucks. So either you bite the bullet and have "the conversation" and find out, or you continue to suffer in silence. I guarantee that by the time you're suffering, the sex will not be as great. Great STD sex can keep your hope pretty high for a while, but this too shall pass. If you are alone in this STD love, be brave and move on. Staying with someone you're in love with, but isn't in love with you, ends up sucking out your lifeblood. You'll also notice your STD works less and less effectively. There will come a time when (shudder to think) you'll be left with...the truth. And the truth is, whoever you are, you deserve to be with someone who is toe-to-toe as in love with you as you are with them.

Seasonal STD

Sunshine and warmth can trigger raging pheromones, especially after a winter spent single or recovering from your last skin adventure/romance. All women look good to me at this point: The cute baby-dyke espresso girl has potential, if not longevity. By the third date she's sure to ask me about a cool lezzie movie she saw about vampires with that French blond actress—have I ever seen it? "Only seven times," I'll tell her. She'll be impressed by my grasp of history, and I'll wonder if it's unethical to sleep with her just one last time. Then there's the type-A tax attorney who's so continually stressed out that she looks like she's wearing shoulder pads even when she isn't. Maybe we could have a tryst. OK, so my arty/freelance ways and modest income will eventually drive her crazy, but who knows what lurks beneath that blue-suit exterior? Seasonal STD has set in.

Bad dates, heartaches, odd affairs—seasonal STD handily takes care of them. It kicks in like clockwork every year, whether I have a girlfriend or not. I dismiss all those inexplicable affairs and brushes with mental illness I've had since the fall as mere flukes, aberrations. If I have a girlfriend, all those frosty "it's the same argument" nights disappear into the long-term storage part of my brain. Spring has indeed sprung and with it a full-on case of STD. Although often joyful, seasonal STD can lead to the other two STDs, and there you are back again, dating the same girl, different haircut.

So, back to my original meditation: At what point does lust turn into love? If I knew exactly, I'd be very wealthy and the host of my very own infomercial. But I do have some thoughts on it. I can tell it's love when: She's not even in the same room (or state for that matter) and I catch myself smiling at something she said…or did. I anticipate seeing her, and my heart gets (oh, God, this is corny) happy. I want to tell her all my funny stories. I listen to every word she says like it's a big treat—all the time. *And* she feels the same way about me. Oh, and I haven't had to make up one bit of her personality. She's totally charming, as is.

part four

Romance

If you're happily in love, there's no point in reading this section. I simply cannot come up with witty essays about the positive side of romance. It's not the kind of thing people commiserate about. Thus, you might consider skipping ahead to Part Six, "The (Gulp) Breakup," just to see what might be in store for you.

The Non-girlfriend Girlfriend

How does one wake up one day and realize she is the non-girlfriend girlfriend? It might not have exactly started out that way, but now is the time for bare-bones honesty. There are three basic ways one gets there: (1) the object of your affection has a primary R (relationship), but the couple is currently separated, so she's technically single; (2) she has a primary "open" R, which means they both have a lover—or three—outside of their sacred union; or (3) she's a lying, cheating sack of…well, you get the picture. She's especially that last one if she doesn't even mention her primary R until *after* you've consummated the affair.

If this were a black-and-white '50s movie, you'd be the "other woman" and for sure would suffer a terrible end: You'd be cast out from decent society, foraging in Dumpsters or devolving into a down-and -out barfly. Fortunately, this is not the '50s, and more than likely you won't have to become a prostitute or hurl yourself off a cliff when you realize your lover went home to the wife—permanently.

I've made out a list of things your beloved will say that are instant tip-offs that you are in fact the non-girlfriend girlfriend:

1. I can't live without you (but I can't break up with her either)!

2. You're my soul mate. I can't let you go!

3. It's just unfinished business—it'll all be over soon.

4. I've *never* had sex like this with anyone!

5. It makes me crazy to think of you with someone else. (This from the person with a joint checking account and mortgage—and not with you.)

6. But her parents adore me—it'd break their hearts!

There are others, but these are the most common, according to my friend Lynnly, who originated the term *non-girlfriend girlfriend* and will not go on record with anything further, except to say that nine times out of 10 the non-GF GF is the fish that gets thrown back. She strongly advises against staying in this situation, no matter how many times the rune/tarot readers and psychic hotlines confirm that you are in fact soul mates. Decide that this must be the lifetime in which she learns that the one she can't live *without* is the one she should be living *with*. Period, end of story.

Simply put, there are almost no happy endings for the non-GF GF. Why do we even go there? I believe it's form of STD (Sexually Transmitted Denial—see my essay on this in Part Three of this book), one in which the non-GF GF has a personality you love, but you're in total denial about the increasing depth of your own feelings and omit anything that counters them. Like reality. Like the fact that though she doesn't mention her primary R but it's always somehow hanging there just at the edge of your conscious. One day your STD will be on vacation and you'll get (argh!) the full picture. One where it's her and her R, front and center and there you are, half cut out of the frame. That's when hopefully you'll take your camera, toothbrush, and sex toys, say goodbye, and mean it.

Rebound Girl: Better to Bounce Than to Break

Most of us have been on one side or the other of this equation. It's one of those inevitable life experiences—unless you found your one true love in high school and have been blissfully in love ever since (collective gag now).

I will focus on the Rebound Girl because she could use a few sympathetic words. First off, the person on the rebound will often omit that fact when dating, since after all, who wants to date the newly scorched? After she has sufficiently seduced you into a pheromonal daze, she may subtly throw into casual conversation, "Oh, I hear Sarah MacLaughlin has a new CD. Did I mention my eight-year relationship ended last month? Could you pass the jam?"

The most extreme case of Rebound Girl happened to my friend Jaylek. After several weeks of E-mailing and chatting on the phone, meeting for coffee, and a few luscious, long kisses, the following conversation ensued:

Her: My girlfriend is moving across the country this Saturday. After that, I'll be officially single.

Jaylek: Huh?

Her: We decided neither of us wanted a long-distance relationship. I wanted to be honest with you. What's wrong?

What's wrong?! my friend wanted to scream. Any honest

person would have told me this little factoid three weeks ago when she started hitting on me! You never once mentioned a girlfriend in the present tense! Jaylek promptly lost all sexual interest in this woman, since deceit is so terribly unattractive.

On one occasion, I was unwittingly being set up as Rebound Girl—she's starting to sound like a superhero: Rebound Girl. She can leap from broken heart to bitter cynicism in a single bound. She can give you that quick-romance fix faster than you can say codependent! Who you gonna call? Ree-Bound Girl!!!

The setup happened at my gym. An especially fit and fetching babe—with whom I was on a gym-friendly nod hello basis—started speaking to me in full sentences. This is a big step in gym culture. You go there four to five times a week and it's your "safe" place. One doesn't want to feel obligated to talk to too many people. You also don't want to strike up a casual conversation with someone who might turn out to be *way* chatty, etc. Anyway, like something you'd see on the Discovery Channel, I circled cautiously, keeping my replies brief. She knew the game and seemed to be subtly adding a sentence or two during our chance encounters—which were growing suspiciously more frequent. My tribal instincts alerted me that something was up, but what?

Sure, she was so strong, with a physique so dazzling that half the gym surreptitiously stole glances as she did her five or more pull-ups unassisted on the Universal. Few women over—or under—the age of 18 can do any pull-ups at all. And she had one of those smiles that made you involuntarily smile back.

Our chats evolved into conversations. Then one day it happened: "Can I work in?" suddenly sounded sexy. Before I could stop myself, I said, "Sure, long as it's our little secret..." She flashed a bashful yet confident smile. She'd successfully ambushed me—mostly because I was a willing dope.

The big day finally arrived when we agreed to go out for smoothies and shots of wheat grass juice. Over said elixirs of love, she mentioned that her seven-year relationship had recently ended. I gagged on my wheat grass juice and realized it really did taste how a freshly mowed yard smells. "I'm sorry...how long ago?"

"Last month." [*Big, pained sigh*]

We both knew, pun intended, that the ball was in my court. It was a crucial moment. Did I like her enough to ignore the intelligent part of my psyche that was screaming, *Run away! Change gyms! You know you'll be Rebound Girl!* Or would I listen to entirely different body parts, the ones screaming, *Life is short! Jump and a net will appear! No pain, no gain!* I realize my body parts talk in clichés and am slightly embarrassed for them.

Needless to say, I jumped. It was grand, and a couple of months later she told me she needed time to herself: She hadn't been completely single in a while and needed to be that, etc. She offered to change her workout schedule if that would be easier for me. I wanted to say, *Could you change it to another state, say Arkansas?* But my psyche chimed in with a gloating *I told you so!* In fairness, I hadn't expected the affair to last long. I did genuinely like her. I did genuinely miss her.

Sometimes a girl's got to do what a girl's got to do. That includes being Rebound Girl, the one who knows how to bounce rather than break.

Falling for the Straight Girl

URGH. Not my most articulate opening, but this one is fraught with stereotypes (i.e., gay people "recruiting" non-gays) and heartache. Now, there are those who, among their gay-girl friends, will say that inside every straight woman is a gay girl dying to get out—if for no other reason than variety. Obviously, the world at large does not *bare* this out, though if the world at large would get over its judgmental self, I do believe there would be many more Sapphic sisters, especially those of the bisexual variety. For the purposes of this essay I am going to focus on my friend, whom we'll name Stacey. Of all my gay-girl friends, she is the one dyke who has consistently fallen for straight girls.

Stacey is an exceptionally cute and athletic butch-identified woman who is fatally attracted to femme straight girls. I must add, this phenomenon is by no means limited to butch gay girls. I also have one femme-identified acquaintance who always falls for some very femme straight woman. The straight-girl love bug can strike any of us at any time. And it's almost never pretty.

Back to Stacey, who's a brown belt in karate (I take this to mean pre-black, but pretty damn good), and meets lots of these straight girls through martial arts or work situations. She clearly doesn't meet them at the local gay bar—though Stacey has admitted to me that more than once, while at a gay-girl event, she has been attracted to the one straight woman in the entire place. Turns out they are generally accompanying a newly out sister or friend and are there just for support. Bravo, you straight girls, for the support—just don't dance most of the night away with a fetching butch without mentioning that you're straight sometime between song one and song 17. To the straight girl, it may be a flattering, unexpected thrill; to the Staceys of the world, it's another failed attempt at meeting the woman of their dreams.

Then there are the straight-girl teases. Sorry, my sister-woman-sisters, but in my presence this has happened to my friend Stacey on more than one occasion. To qualify, there are probably just as many gay-girl teases, but somehow the truth hurts more when you had assumed they were changing their sexual object choice just because you're so darn adorable. It works like this: Stacey will invite them to do something innocuous together, say a hike or lunch at a cool café, and sometime during these exchanges the straight girl will start to flirt with Stacey. At first Stacey will think she's imagining it, but when said straight girl breaks a date with her "loser boyfriend" (in her words) to watch videos with Stacey, it makes a girl think. They'll start to sit closer and closer on the couch, then OUCH! Gotta go, thanks for the popcorn! As she runs off into the heterosexual night.

Another scenario is the "I was drunk and can't remember" type of woman. I saw this one in action. This supposedly straight buddy of Stacey's who knew Stacey had a crush on her—they had even talked about it—was hanging all over Stacey at this club like it was the honeymoon suite. I even took Stacey aside for a little chat.

"What is up with Sheila?" I asked her. "I thought she was straight."

"I don't know, but I'm liking it fine."

"Stacey, be careful. You know how this goes. How many Long Islands has that woman had? I think two is the legal limit, and three is the 'It's all your lesbian fault time.' "

True to form, Stacey drove her home (I cabbed it earlier). They made out for about a half-hour, then Sheila conveniently passed out. The next day, Stacey didn't know what to do. The night before, this woman had been all over her like hot fudge on vanilla ice cream. Stacey, being an honorable sort, had initially pushed her away and asked her if she knew what she was doing, etc. Sheila replied nonverbally. When Stacey called her the next day, the machine was on—always a bad sign. Then, two days later when they talked, Sheila was all giggles: Didn't she tie one on, huh?

Stacey was crushed. Not again. Did these straight women think she has no feelings? That these flings meant nothing to her? Unfortunately, it might have been that they have confused Stacey with straight men, who may never call the woman or even care that there was that "closer communication time" at the end of the evening—OK, I can already hear protests: of course not *all* straight men, but certainly those of the "meet, greet, bed, and goodbye" variety. Now Stacey would have to change her dojo, again.

In fairness, there are women who don't come out until a bit later in life, so someone's got to help them along. Many of these women come into their gay-girl selves with great joy and abandon. Others suffer in the valley of the damned from internalized homophobia, and being their first lover can be a real challenge. Me? I've never had any desire to be the gay welcome wagon, though when I was an undergrad a few straight women hit on me. It was always some babe in my women studies class. It always involved too much alcohol and always occurred at the end of the semester. That way they didn't have to avoid me in class or vice versa. Lest one would think me overly virtuous, yes, I'd be their date for the night, but I harbored no illusions that one night with me and they'd jump willy-nilly into the gay-girl world. One of these women, however, did eventually come out; I met her years later at a gay-girl bar in (surprise) San Francisco.

Other than those few experiences (three to be exact), flattering though it may be, I refuse to be that one taste of the exotic, the forbidden. It isn't sexy to me. I swear it's not ethics, because if my pheromones got in a tussle and she was doing the asking, I'd give it a try. But so far it hasn't been that way for me. And of course I no longer drink the way so many of us did in college. Still, I'm not one to tempt fate with absolutes. You know you'll get nailed once you start any sentence with the words "I'll never date a therapist, a 20-something, a portfolio carrier, a deb type, or any fill-in-the-blank again." The universe will immediately deliver that person on your doorstep, simply loaded with pheromonal activity and a huge crush on you. That said, if sometime it turns out that a heretofore heterosexual woman is the woman of my dreams *and* she's very crushed out on me, then I would consider a long, *slowww* romantic courtship.

What about Stacey? I'm happy to say that as of this writing, she yet again started up another friendship-plus with a straight woman, but this time they fell madly in love and are now living together in gay-girl bliss in the suburbs.

Saint Valentine, Where Art Thou?

It's February, and it's dreary. Gray has more hues now than in any other month, and we're all sick of—or with—the flu. OK, maybe not the folks in Miami. The one bright spot, other than President's Day (a day off work), is of course Saint Valentine's Day. Curious, I did a bit of research on Saint Valentine. Ex–Roman Catholics simply cannot resist this kind of thing. Turns out Valentine was a martyr executed in Rome in 270 C.E. Now, what could be more romantic? The only martyrs I remember are from my Catholic school days (yes, another gay girl who went to school with the nuns). They were on "holy cards" being tortured to death in full Technicolor. These were my role models when I was growing up. If you won a spelling bee, you got someone burning or bleeding to death as your prize. Great incentive, huh? Oh, and the cards were laminated in plastic so they'd last a good long time.

I decided early on that I had no aspirations to have my own personal holy card depicting my agonizing death. Martyrs—not the sharpest knives in the drawer, they. Think about it, they're asked a simple question, like "Do you believe in this Christian God?" They could have just lied—if God is omnipotent, you only have to let him know in your head that you believe in him, and for sure he'll get the message, right? But no, they have to tell the truth, so they answer, "Yep. Absolutely."

"You know we're going to stone you to death unless you change your mind?"

"Nope, not going to change my mind."

Hence the reward many centuries later of appearing on a holy card.

Given my religious background, I had to wonder, *Why a martyr?* But the more I thought about it, the more I realized that I myself have had more than one "romantic" adventure that had a burning or bleeding-to-death quality.

Interestingly, another definition for Valentine is "a town in northern Nebraska." Now, there's a town that's a whole lot more fun than Groundhog, Nebraska. All the same, Valentine's Day is a holiday that requires a fair amount of prep work. It can also be a stressful time. A friend of mine, when single on the Big V for the third year in a row, threw a black Saint Valentine's party. Everyone was instructed to wear black clothes and only dark-colored food and beverages were served (that ended up being chocolate, Guinness, chocolate, merlot, chocolate, Pepsi, and more chocolate). Everyone ended up relatively nauseated, with a vague sense of having avenged something, though no one ever quite figured out what.

Since nobody can really escape this holiday, I've devised the following quiz. You may choose as many answers as you like.

What's Your Valentine's Day IQ?

1. If you're in a budding relationship, you will most likely:

    (a) Spend half your paycheck buying your gal the most exquisite flowers available in North America (especially if you haven't slept together yet).

    (b) Spend the other half of your paycheck on Victoria's not-so-Secret or Calvin "we all have puffy lips models" Klein garment-lets.

    (c) Make dinner reservations before you finish reading this or you'll be eating at the palace d'amour: Sizzler.

    (d) Do nothing—let her take care of everything.

2. If you're single, you will most likely:

    (a) Ignore the holiday; it will go away, and then all that candy will be half price.

    (b) Wear every shade of red you own to prove to one and all that being single doesn't bother you a bit. And it doesn't. Really.

    (c) Live on bags of individually wrapped, heart-shaped Butterfinger bars indefinitely or until you require bridge work.

    (d) Move to Miami.

3. If you're in a long-term relationship or married, you will probably:

    (a) Make a pact with your lover to save the flower and candy money for your next Home Depot excursion.

133

(b) Accidentally buy the exact same card as last year because it's so perfect for your lover (and you're a bit absent-minded).

(c) Forget to make a dinner reservation (because you didn't read my column, perhaps?), end up ordering out pizza and watching a pay-per view movie at home.

(d) Offer to give your partner a full-body massage. When your partner counter-offers to trade and insists on giving you one first, you accept and just before it's finished you promptly fall into a deep blissful sleep.

4. **If you're not sure which dating/relationship category you're in:**
   (a) Ask yourself the tough questions: Do we kiss? Do we call each other pumpkin head? Do I know her last name?

   (b) Call your friends to see if anyone's noticed anything unusual.

   (c) Consider you're way too busy if you have no idea whether you're single, married or dating.

   (d) How did you even *get* to this question?

How to Score Yourself:
- a's are worth 5 points each.
- b's are worth 12 points each.
- c's are worth 3.2 points each.
- d's are worth 127 points each.

If you scored over 400, you have some serious work to do in the romance department. And quite frankly, you probably already knew "the score," so act accordingly.

Now that you know your V-Day IQ, here's a cautionary tale about one truly miserable V-Day I spent with the object of my great affections. It's all about planning and the fact that we've all been convinced that the fancier the restaurant the deeper the love.

For weeks said lover, Isabelle, keeps calling me and asking where I want to go for Valentine's Day. As this is a long-distance relationship and I am flying down, I consistently reply, "Honey, you live in Santa Barbara—you decide." I arrive. No reservations have been made. I'm not upset. I'd be happy eating pizza with her in the bathtub. But, no, my GF is a traditionalist. We are going to prove our gay-girl love to the world. After hours of calling restaurants, we find one that will take us: "On the porch, it's really nice...special for Valentine's Day." I'm suspicious, but since it was on the A-list supplied by her (richer) friends, Isabelle is thrilled.

We arrive and are placed at an outdoor table, complete with New Orleans-style heat lamps and plastic floor-to-ceiling tarps. We decide, nonverbally, that this will be fine (it's either this or Taco Bell). The chairs are those plastic white outdoor kind. Ouch. We're all dressed up in our silky best, wearing makeup, cool shoes—the works. And we're sitting on chairs we wouldn't buy on sale.

It's a prix fixe menu with four choices (two meat, one fish, one vegetarian—this is California). My GF insists on treating since she was the one to wait until the last minute, and I flew down. If we were more butch/femme–identified, this would be a nonissue. The butch pays (and a good butch makes those reservations early—but more on that another time). On the B/F scale with 1 being super femme, never without her Nordstrom card, and 10 being stone butch, never far from a tool kit, she's butch of center (7) and I'm femme of center (3). So who pays is really a toss-up.

So I let her prevail and be the butch, which I know she enjoys. More than 20 minutes passes before a waitress approaches us, which gives us time to scope out the porch "dining" area. Within 10 minutes a lesbian couple and their 12-year-old daughter are seated catty-corner to us. Before the end of the meal, yet another lesbian couple will be seated downstairs on the porch. Coincidence? Possibly. Of course, if we were gay men we'd have reserved a well-placed table in July.

Our waitress is phony nice, of the "I'm in a hurry and I'm doing you a favor coming all the way out here to serve you" variety. I do not make fun of waitresses lightly, being an ex-waitress myself. But this woman clearly lost the coin toss and got…us: the porch people. Isabelle speaks fluent French and unconsciously corrected our waitress's pronunciation twice. I let her order for me just to hear her say "filet mignon" in French. A petty but satisfying revenge on the waitress. Our appetizers of tiny but delicious crabcakes arrive after 40 minutes. I'd have eaten Hot Pockets on rice at that point. Still, they were quite tasty, though far too nouvelle (read: teensy).

Our entrées arrive. I had requested my filet mignon meat medium rare. My vegan/vegetarian sisters can skip this next part. The moment I graze it with my knife, there's blood all over my plate. And it's cold. I send it back. Our fellow porch dwellers ignore us. Oh, well, so much for solidarity. My steak returns cooked all the way through. I accept it anyway, knowing this is the best they are going to do. My partner's N.Y. T-Bone turns out to be fatty and full of grizzle. When we are finished with our meal, a neat stack of the inedible meat is stacked on my GF's plate.

Our waitress approaches. "Did everything work out?" she asks.

"Actually, no," I reply. "My steak was well-done, and hers was barely edible."

I wait her out. She says nothing, rapidly clearing the wreckage of our meal. Finally, with a big smile, she encouragingly offers, "We have great desserts!" as she rushes off to a nicer table.

Twenty minutes later, over what turns out to be great desserts and coffee, I hear my lover mutter, "That was the stupidest $200 I ever spent." I cringe. Two hundred dollars?! At least we get to go home now.

The moral of the story? Never, I mean NEVER try to get into a "good" restaurant for Saint Valentine's Day on Saint Valentine's Day. If you are able to get a reservation, be suspicious. The depth of your love is not contingent on the price of your meal. Better you should make an extravagant meal in your sexiest undergarment-lets than be pissed off and $200 lighter.

Now, as I mentioned re the black Valentine's Day party, being single can either take a machete to your self-esteem or be an opportunity for growth. I must admit even when I have a girlfriend/date, I find the forced romance of it all to be a high-pressure situation. I'll bet plenty of people break up from a botched Valentine's Day. If there's a crack in the relationship to begin with, all that romantic hyperbole puts a wedge in it. The relationship's inadequacies come pouring out.

In recent memory, I've been totally single on two St. Valentine's Days: 1997 and 2000. But what's wrong with that? It's always been my firm conviction that there's no shame in being single. Sure, if it goes on too long, "sex for one" can become physically injurious (use your imagination—better yet, don't). At that point, one should be using all that excess energy for the good of humanity, or at least in an exercise regime. And get out of the house: see local theater productions, go to live sports events, volunteer somewhere, or take advantage of cheap airfares. Remember, anyone can be in a sick relationship anytime they want. There will always be someone sicker than you out there who will be more than happy to fill your days and nights (mostly with chaos, but that's your choice). Never let any holiday convince you that because you're single, clearly there's something wrong with you. Think of it as fighting yet another insidious societal control aimed at lowering your self-esteem, like all the impossibly thin popular female movie stars. I think Drew Barrymore and Kate Winslet are the only two sex symbol–type stars who look like they ate their entire sandwich (with chips). I thank you both. If one of them were single on V-Day, I bet she'd find a way to have fun, wreak havoc, or at least settle in with a good book.

Redressing Your Lover

This essay may appear to be the height of triviality, a gross manifestation of our consumer culture and all the rest of that (and it is), but what do you do when you've fallen for a bad dresser (or haircut)? I'm aware that "bad" is an extremely subjective term, especially when applied to fashion sense or lack thereof. And I must admit a kind of fondness for those truly oblivious that the '80s *and* '90s are in fact over. There is a kind of absent-minded, lack-of-vanity quality that can be quite charming. But when she's wearing those cover-half-your-face glasses in public, and they are not retro '70s cool, what do you do? It's fine for moms or grandmoms but not your lover! It's frightening, quite frankly. She wasn't wearing them when you met. It's all you can do not to run to the nearest hip eyeglass emporium and shell out the requisite $400 yourself. But how do you do this without hurting your beloved's feelings?

I've collected stories from my friends, and they all redressed at least one lover. One friend—we'll call her Chris—was actually smitten with a woman with one of those hairdo "tails" circa 1983. The short haircut with a two-foot strand of hair running down the back? Chris didn't even see it at first. And this was only five years ago. Apparently, the woman started growing it when she was 13 as an act of rebellion and never got over it. Chris moved very slowly but firmly. She respected that there was an emotional, symbolic value attached to said tail but felt embarrassed in public for her lover and by association herself. She felt terrible that she was being so shallow, but she had to get rid of that tail.

Her first thought was to point out other cute dyke do's when they were out and about. Her lover would agree in a vague way: "Yes, cute." Clearly, her lover didn't want to be awakened from her long "hair do's and don'ts" sleep. So my friend took it to the next level: Lead by example. Chris got a brand new short and tousled do herself. The lover thought it was very cute. Seizing this opening, Chris rhapsodized about how good it felt to have a whole different look. It was now or never, so Chris bravely, but with calculated casualness, pressed the issue. The conversation went something like this:

Chris: Sweetie, how about you? Time for a new do?

Entailed lover: Why? I like my hair. Don't you?

Chris: Well, no.

Entailed lover: What's the difference? I'm a dyke for God's sake. I don't have to live up to male-dominated fashion standards!

Chris: True, but...it's...the...tail thing.

Entailed lover: MY TAIL! I've had it for practically as long as I can remember. That'd be like changing my eyes from brown to blue or something.

Chris: : No, it wouldn't—that's what's so great about hair: You can do all this great stuff with it, even if you are a dyke. I'm a dyke, and I didn't change my hair for some white male capitalist in the sky. I did it because change is good, and because I'm not the same person I was three years ago—or even last month.

Chris was especially pleased with that last argument. Her lover conceded the point and said she'd think about it. In the end her lover shaved her head completely—to get a really fresh perspective. Chris saw this as a big step up from the tail and bought her lover a cute knit cap to keep her head warm.

Then there's the "Where do they even find these dated styles that look new?" clothing aspect. Is there a warehouse in New Jersey where lesbians can pick up new multicolored silk blouses, leg warmers, and drawstring pants? In the mid '90s another friend of mine—let's call her Lauren (none of my friends want to go on the record with these stories because they don't want to hurt their exes' feelings)—dated a professional-type woman who turned up at a cultural outing wearing a blouse that had that strap that buttoned up the sleeve to 3/4's length. And it was buttoned up. To add insult to injury, her date exclaimed how a friend of hers gave her all this great clothing: "Like this shirt—can you believe she was going to throw this out?" Lauren claims she wanted to scream, "Yes! The last time I saw one of those shirts, Reagan was in office and I was in high school!" But her date was such a sweet woman—though someone in desperate need of, well, not a makeover, more of an updating, at least into the present decade.

Even as I write this I feel like, "Who died and left me fashion czar?" I know I have my moments when suddenly I look around and notice I'm the only person wearing "X." And some things I'm stubborn about—like my total resistance to current hip-style gym clothing. But to me that doesn't count somehow, because I'm not out in the world, though technically the gym

141

is a public place, and there's probably been more than one gay girl who's spied me in the gym and decided, "Cute biceps, but where'd she get the outfit? The Great Depression?"

I think it comes down to how much you like the woman and how bad her fashions really are. If you're in love but try to talk her out of going to your softball game because you're scared she's going to wear one of her sweatshirts that has that rubbery, actually raised-off-the-fabric, overly colorful print on it, you need to talk. Or better yet, at every gift-giving opportunity, give her clothing you bought locally (not from that warehouse in New Jersey).

The Mean One (Or, How Did I End Up Wrong AGAIN?!)

Everyone eventually will have a date, affair, romance or even a (gasp!) relationship with the type of person I call the Mean One (TMO). They are out there, both literally and figuratively. Eventually, it becomes apparent that she's got a mean streak so wide you could drive a 4x4 through it. OK, technically that'd be "on" it, but that's not as dramatic, and one thing these couplings always include is drama—*big* drama. And you thought those days were over. On the upside, once you've figured out she's TMO, you only have one option: Get out! For reasons best left to trained mental health professionals, many of us are drawn, at least for a while (or until we loose every shred of self-respect), to someone who is difficult, contrary, and often downright mean. All because of this blind hope that once you win her over, she'll change. You're that special person who understands, and what you both felt was so great at the beginning that it must still be there somewhere. You won't, she won't, and it's gone forever.

First, you must learn how to spot the Mean One. Now, this is not as easy as it sounds, because most of them start out all charm, seduction, and this is *so* unique and special. This feels great, and dopes that we are, we believe them. And why not? They seem to be the whole package: bright, sexy, and they adore you. What could be wrong? You'll find out once she knows she's got you ensnared in her evil vortex of lopsided romance. Subtly but surely, you'll start to notice that every-thing has shifted to being on her terms: where and when you'll meet and for how long, who calls who, and most importantly, how involved she can get. The latter will usually progress from special and unique to the vortex of "I can't get too emo-tionally involved; I'm not ready for a girlfriend; I'm in an open relationship" to "Let's just see how it goes." All her statements more than suggest that you'd better follow suit, or for sure one day she'll be able to say with impunity, "I warned you. I was always honest with you. I didn't mean to hurt you. That's why I was straight up about how I felt." And she did *say* those things, but she also said and *did* a lot of other stuff in the other direction: the occasional thoughtful gift; the sly, sexy look given while others are present and it's your big secret; the passionate sex followed by long, meaningful but unartic-ulated looks. This is definitely a time when the old adage "Actions speak louder than words" might be applied. But somehow when you get into these discussions you can't come up with any tangible examples, and by the end of it all, the score is TMO: 100, you: -16. How does this happen? Over the course of her lifetime, TMO has so finely honed her casual and knee-jerk manipulation that you could cut diamonds with it—or better, perform cardiovascular surgery.

My very own (single) TMO went whole-hog after me with sprays of flowers and the sweetest looks imaginable. She told me she loved me after a mere two weeks; it took me a little longer to agree. (I essentially did a "Me too.") I was seduced by her sureness of our love—oh, and all that sex. My first clue should have been when she made a point of telling me *again* how this gay girl, then that one too, had a crush on her. By crush number 4, I gave her a stony look. Her response was to explain to me that in this society she was the one in the couple who had what was considered good looks. It's fucked up, she said, but that's how it is. And it happens to her all the time—no big deal. Oh, and I shouldn't let it bother me—it isn't like she cares.

I was stunned. I knew I had just been insulted, but I wasn't sure exactly how. I thought I had every right to give her a cold "Not this again—fuck-you" look but ended up feeling ugly and unworldly. If I'd been more sophisticated, I'd have seen the situation for its screwy social implications, which were some straight white guy's fantasy anyway. I was young. Now I can see clearly that the implication was that she was the good-looking one and *moi* the average "Who would even glance your way?" one. Her constantly mentioning other girls was designed to keep me off-balance and to appreciate what a knockout I had somehow hooked against all odds. Remember, she romanced me. Three months later she cheated on me—publicly. I know she enjoyed it. At that point, I did get out, even as she protested loudly that she was a sex-and-love addict and never meant to hurt me—she loved me! Hadn't she told me at the beginning that she had a problem with cheating? But she also said she was working on her issues very seriously. I naively took that to mean she wouldn't cheat on me. She had assured me that this was different, special. But hadn't she warned me, she demanded to know, as I packed all my "overnight things" that had accumulated in her apartment. This didn't mean she loved me less, only that she had intimacy issues!

I've only experienced one other TMO, and I made quick work of her. It had been less than a month when I realized she was all smiles and charm to the young woman making our espresso but offhand and abrupt with me. I don't think so. That night, I told her this dating situation wasn't working out for me. I was older and saw her coming before she even got a chance to bring out the heavy artillery.

Another kind of TMO is the woman in an open relationship, or just getting out of one, or on a break from one, etc. A good friend of mine was on a documentary film shoot in the wilds of New Zealand when she was seduced by this particular kind of TMO. Granted, she was probably the only gay girl within a hundred or more miles, but still, my friend could have been in the middle of the Castro and she would have gone for it. This woman was that good. Her TMO, as usual, was more than ordinarily good-looking, clever, and had that hypersexiness that wafted off her like a vapor of demonic proportions. Given the location and boys' club environment of a film shoot, no one would think it odd that they'd pal around. Since half the crew were New Zealanders and not nearly so at ease with gay girls as their U.S. counterparts, their affair would for sure need to be discreet. True, any crew/set romance should be on the quiet side (unless you're Meg Ryan and Russell Crowe), because you all work together 12–16 hours a day and it's in bad form to complicate or throw off the group dynamics. But discretion is especially important for the safety and job security of gay girls.

All that said, after one of the crew end-of-the-day beers, TMO asks to check out my friend's trailer. On film shoots, especially on location in the wilderness, everyone is put up in trailers, the privacy and relative condition of which are contingent upon where someone lies in the film food chain. For instance, the director and producer each got their own pretty deluxe trailer, while my friend, a second-second (assistant director), had to share her trailer with the first second or "key" second. The shower smelled of sewage half the time, and the water was undrinkable and smelled like rotten eggs. So, obviously, my friend wasn't that high up on the food chain—somewhere higher than protozoa but lower than plankton. TMO knew the key second had headed off with the boys to check out the local pub, just 40 miles down the road, so my friend's trailer would be empty.

My friend could barely breathe by the time they got inside. The sexual tension had been building for close to two weeks. As my friend fumbled with the beverage issue, this woman, as she rubs my friend's neck says, "I'm in a open relationship, so this is OK…?"

"You're in a relationship?" my friend asks.

TMO pulls her close. "Five years…but we haven't been much on the lovers end of it the last two years. That's why it's open. That all right with you?"

By now they're practically lip to lip. What was my friend going to do? It was kiss her or die of abject desire on the spot. She did what all of us have or would do—she jumped off that cliff and enjoyed every stolen but technically ethical minute. What is it about clandestine sex that is so wonderfully nasty and delicious? A remote location, the need for secrecy, doing it with sweaty abandon until you hear that truck drive up… Then it changes.

After a week of furious, furtive passion, my friend asks TMO if she wants to walk down the trail a bit before the sun goes down—wink, wink. TMO mumbles something about needing to get some paperwork done (she's the location manager). My friend is disappointed but understands. It's a pretty grueling shoot and she's better off with a long shower and more sleep anyway. The next day it's almost back to the usual—the double entendres, the casual touch in passing, the random meetings at the catering table...except something's off-kilter.

My friend: Is something up?

TMO: No. Why?

My friend: You seem—I don't know—different.

TMO: I talked to Julie last night, and I've been honest with you, right? I mean, this is just what it is for right now?

My friend: Ah, well, yes, but are you saying this is sex as sport or something?

TMO: Don't be crass. I just don't want you having feelings I can't reciprocate, that's all.

My friend was stunned. What about all those long looks— "deep into our very-souls" looks—the contraband gifts, the incredible luck to be on the same shoot? Trying to save face, my friend just mumbled something like, "Fun while it lasted."

Later that week, TMO, after an especially hard day—bug bites, rain, you name it—offered my friend a massage at her trailer, saying her roommate would be out. Then she added, "But if you think that'll lead to umm, getting together, I don't want to hurt you..." What to do, what to do? My friend went back with TMO, they did the wild thing, and when my friend started to feel lousy about it, TMO piped in with, "I'm sorry—haven't I been honest with you?" There was nothing my friend could say. TMO had set her up, knocked her down, and blamed it on her.

Immediately after this, I got a long phone call from my friend that put her back at least a month's rent. After hearing all the details (and it is in the details—most of life, that is), I had to inform my friend that she'd just had an affair with The Mean One. TMO had all her fun, had gotten everything her way, and she'd go back to her nice safe relationship and onto the next shoot and the next special and unique gay girl, who won't be my friend.

Please, I beg all TMOs out there: Go seek out your own kind and explode in a frenzy of manipulations and quick fixes! But no, a TMO would never date her own kind. She'll find another naive, hopeless romantic who'll believe in her. She'll get better and better at it, unless she truly has that moment of clarity that sends her into deep therapy. But until then let's hope her next target is not you or me. And even if we are, we now know how to head her off at the pass without pushing her off. Violence creates such bad karma, and she *so* doesn't deserve it—causing you bad vibes, that is; the push off the cliff I'm not so sure about.

She Said the L-Word, I Said the L-Word— Are We in a Relationship?

Love. That state of calm excitement, that wonderful combination of raging pheromones, caring, trust, and the X-factor which defies articulation, though everyone keeps trying nonetheless. One of the telltale signs of encroaching "falling in L—" is that you'll start to think in bad metaphors, clichés, and hokey verbiage. Love is even so wonderful and unique that it's one of the few emotions that comes with directional phrases: You can fall *in* love, or you can fall *out* of love. But no matter which direction you're moving, it's one the greatest markers of being fully alive or at least conscious (though in those first heady stages, it might be an altered state of consciousness). And generally there's no turning back.

By that I mean, one of you will finally say what has probably been obvious for at least five minutes to two weeks. If the other person says it back in kind, it's official. You are in L-O-V-E. That means you are two of the lucky ones (at least for now). In my experience that means you are moments away from being in an R (relationship). It goes with the territory. Let me stress again—*moments,* minutes, maybe a week on the outside. Not that there's anything wrong with being in an R. In my experience, there are many pluses to being in a relationship (see, I can say it), but there's also the reality of commitment and working at keeping a relationship going. So, "I love you" is not an expression to be chosen lightly, or for the sheer wonder of it while in a state of post-coital bliss.

To me, love is the thing. The only thing really, when all is said and done. Not simply romantic love, but all its different manifestations. Believe me, if you died tomorrow, none of your family members or friends would go to your funeral and say, "I really loved her, but she never owned a house, bought a brand-new car, won the Pulitzer, sang on Broadway, or screened at Cannes." Nope. In the end it's only love, kindness, and compassion that will matter, and as my friend Karla's mom says, as she gets older she's figured out this life thing, and one thing's for sure: None of us is getting out alive. So act accordingly.

Back to relationships—why do they so many times start to take on lives of their own? As if you could meet a "relationship" on the bus one day and find out it has its own group of friends, a decent job, and a desire to learn tai chi? Can you tell this makes me nervous? Possibly because my own relationship-longevity track record has not been stupendous, though I've always resented that the validity of a relationship is so often based on quantity not quality. True, the short-lived relationship (say under two years), generally doesn't scream out fabulous "quality" relationship, but there's still something there that annoys me. It's the smugness of some (not all) couples who've been together for over 10 years. That sigh of "Poor Mo, another lover gone wrong."

How come I don't get some points for trying? Not everyone meets her soul mate in high school (probably playing field hockey or basketball, of course…) and lives happily ever after. OK, maybe no one meets her soul mate in high school, but you get the idea.

Being in love *is* all it's cracked up to be and more, if it's the right person and not some delusional wish-fulfillment situation. This happens more than one would like to think. Falling in love with the idea of falling in love is very tempting. And why not? It's the most preferred state of being. It's easier to do than you might think. Say your perfectly adorable dating/lover falls in love with you. You're not exactly sure you feel the same, but you do like her an awful lot and your pheromones are screaming, *She's a keeper!* Pheromones are notoriously self-centered and will do anything to get their way. Think of them as all id with no tempering superego. For those not familiar with Freud's basic theory: The id is made up of unbridled hedonistic urges with no social conscience or awareness of consequences. (Think infant: *I want shiny pointy-thing—knife—NOW, wahhh.*) Superego is sort of the mom/dad, authority/society consciousness. (Think guilt: *I should have done X, but I'm such a fuck-up…*) The battle of these two form your ego or self.

If you're not sure whether you're in love, 99% of the time you're not. Falling in love is simply not to be negotiated. It is or it isn't. Sure, we've all heard that love can grow and all that. And sure, it happens. But rarely. The best test is to break contact for a week with the lover you're not sure you're in love with. Do you think about her all the time? Can you almost not wait to tell her this great story you just heard? Do you miss her so much it hurts—physically hurts? Or after the first four days of body detox, do you start to notice how cute that girl on the Lifecycle is? It's death by fire, but be a trooper. Falling in love with the idea of love is no day at the beach, mall, spa, or your choice of location.

Despite all of the above disclaimers, if you know you're in love, I say you should go for the romance: Treasure it *now* and call it a day—a very good, exceptional day.

part five

The Relationship

- when to have one
- when you're in one
- when one is not enough

The Monogamy Game

What's all this we keep hearing about gay/queer marriage? Clearly, the movement to legalize queer marriage is a big vote for monogamy, since by its very definition marriage means "you to the exclusion of all others." And there are all those handy tax breaks. I'm all for gay marriage—being an artist, I'd love to eventually hone in on someone's health insurance benefits. In San Francisco, that means I have to marry (or become a "domestic partners" with—a phrase that rankles me, but more on that later) a woman in uniform (cop, firefighter, bus driver, etc.) or someone who works for Levi Strauss. Since I apparently only attract women with a lot of personality and no steady income, that is unlikely to happen.

On the other hand there's the decades-old argument against queer marriage: It mimics heterosexual "mores." Now, I realize marriage is not for everyone, but apparently it is for most people, at least for one stretch of their lives. And marriage is not a new concept. Ancient civilizations were drawing out their own domestic situations (kill a beast, feed the kids, women have breasts, men have penises, etc.) on cave walls and such, and these were not people who ever uttered the words, "I have issues." Granted, they probably slept around with both sexes since no one was exactly sure how babies were made, but they did form family units. And of course there was no TV, hence no daytime talk shows, so who knew?

American society goes a long way to validate heterosexual unions with huge weddings and diamond-studded anniversary celebrations. Granted, everyone I know who has planned a traditional huge wedding wants to kill their beloved at least three or four times during the preparations. By wedding's eve they are convinced that this is the litmus test to see if they really want to spend the rest of their lives with this person. I have a secret belief that all this celebration occurs because at some level everyone knows how hard it is to be faithful for the rest of your life to one person to the exclusion of all others. Hence, we might as well get all dressed up, have some great food, and hit the open bar.

But with queers, we have no bolstering media messages that say "Give her a diamond to let her know you'd marry her all over again" or "Send her flowers." Come to think of it, most of the advertising is pretty sexist—why not buy *him* flowers? Nor do we have the legal status or rituals to help out the committed. Now, that sounds attractive: the committed—about as romantic as "domestic partners." For me, the latter always brings to mind images of taking out the garbage or arguing over who scrubbed the tub or ate the last of the Smart Start cereal. I realize that "domestic partners" was probably chosen to prove how utterly normal and boring most gay people are, or at least in approximately the same percentages as our straight counterparts.

Marriage. Till death do us part. That's enough to scare anyone—gay or straight. It's that happy-go-lucky death thing. It reminds of the cover of one issue of *The Advocate* that displayed two gay men in bed with the radical headline, "Monogamy: Is It For Us?" Now, I presume they intended the question to include lesbians, but let's face it, monogamy is a nonissue for 90% of all lesbians, whereas the reverse could be said for gay men—i.e., 90% of gay men understand the concept theoretically, but how it applies to them personally is a tad more problematic. The article had one very bizarre scientific fact that got me going.

Factoid #1: Evolutionary scientists have argued for years that since sperm is cheap and plentiful, males want to spread their "seed" as much as possible, whereas with females, eggs are limited and precious, so they are much more cautious with their sexual encounters. Now, I have to admit, this makes some sense, regardless of sexual orientation. Particularly when it's abundantly clear in the queer community that most gay girls tend to get the hang of monogamy with barely a blip on the radar screen, while most gay men fight the concept tooth -and well-manicured nail. And to qualify, I also know lots of gay guys who adore falling in love, some for a week, some for a month. OK, I do know one gay male couple who've been together 16 years. But the majority of my gay boyfriends fall into the three-months to three-year category (and that doesn't include random sexual encounters). Come to think of it, I fall into that last category too. Hmmmm. Perhaps, I have a gay-male gene? Xq28, anyone?

Then there are the tried but true aspects of long-term monogamy. I've been known to refer to this as the "tired and blue" phase. You know monogamy has taken a turn for the monotonous when you're invited to a long-term couple's place for dinner and have that same smoked salmon pasta with the baby greens salad for the third time running. Maybe that's what they serve to any guest on a Friday evening.

Saturday is usually Chinese takeout, and every single time one of them comments, "I love this garlic eggplant! Don't you?" You want to scream, "Enough about the eggplant! What about politics, that quirky indie film, the latest gay-girl celebrity scandal?" You love your friends, but some LTRs get into a kind of holding pattern that makes you crazy.

For me, it goes a long way to reassure my gay-male gene that says the "three months to three years" relationship style may not be so awful. But then again, I may not have chanced upon someone I could find endlessly charming, sexy, and fun.

Blame it on Hollywood, the media, my eggs, but I think most of us would be delighted to be madly, passionately in love for years and years. We could skip all the stuff that keeps us so emotionally busy: dates or no dates, romance or lust, being monogamous or open, staying together or breaking up. Think of all the free time you'd have to start that project, plan unusual outings, treasure that person who makes your heart so happy. Sigh. In the meantime, however, a girl's got to have some fun.

Meeting Her Parents (Or, It's All Relative)

"Relatives: Merely a noisy pack of people who haven't the least inkling of how to live, nor the good sense to know when to die." Roughly paraphrased from the great Oscar Wilde, whose own cynicism masked a deep romanticism. I could not resist opening this essay with so tasty a quote. There are three types of parents: PFLAG parents, the "don't bother to come home until you get over this gay thing" parents, and the parents who are trying but everything they know about gay people they learned on Jerry Springer. With increasingly queer visibility, it is a bit easier for many of us, though most of that visibility still seems to lean heavily toward good-looking, white males who never visibly have sex (but they do pal around with that nice straight woman). Which, of course, does not help out the gay girl much in matters of the family.

It seems that many first meetings take place during the holidays, when sibling attendance is required—i.e., Christmas, Hanukkah, or Kwanza. It is a time of glad tidings, good will, love, and all that, though it's actually the most stressful time of the year (ask any paramedic). So amidst the anxiety, busy schedules, shopping, travel arrangements, and crazed cooking, you're going to bring your new beloved home to meet the family. It's wise to note that you two are not exempt from any of the above either. So tread carefully and carry a copy of one of Ellen DeGeneres's mom's books. I've never actually read one, but she looks so momish on the cover, who could she possibly scare? And if that doesn't work, hit your brother in the head with it if he makes one more crack like, "You were always a tomboy—how'd you get such a cute babe?" Apparently, sibling rivalry doesn't end until you're so old that you don't have the energy or verbal command left to torture another human being who shares your DNA. You'll save it up for the Social Security people who keep saying "There's simply no money! Remember that $300 you got back in 2000? That was it." But I (again) digress.

Let's start with the card-carrying PFLAG parents. They will go out of their way to treat you and your lover exactly like your heterosexual married siblings—so much so that you may start to feel like you're in a Lifetime movie of the week. You'll hear the phrase, "you two" so often you'll want to scream. ("What are *you two* going to do on New Year's Eve?" "Could *you two* run and pick up two more quarts of eggnog? Uncle Charlie is coming." "How are *you two* finding the guest bedroom? OK, I hope.") Granted, this is much better than the "don't step a foot in this house until you come to your senses" parents. Still, with PFLAG parents you and your girl will start to feel a bit like poster children for the lesbian nation and you'll have an uncontrollable urge to do the nation proud (then later resent it). But you are getting the best end of it, so enjoy.

The "no daughter of mine is a lesbian" kind of parents are sort of a nonissue because, well, who would bother even trying in that situation? Why put yourself and your girlfriend through it? That your parents, together or apart, are staunchly entrenched in a particularly hateful way of thinking is probably not going to change when you ring that doorbell. Perhaps sending them a copy of the Ellen's coming-out episode will grease the wheels of their brains a little. People can surprise you. There are those who brazenly show up with their partner to help destigmatize the whole thing. To those women, I bid Godspeed. I don't exactly know what that phrase means, but I've heard it in British history–type movies, and it seems to mean good luck, with an extra kick of divine backing.

Now to my personal favorite, the Jerry Springer–type parents and relatives. This would be my family, actually my mom and relatives. My father doesn't count because he's a monk—really—a Christian brother in a monastery in West Virginia. It's a long story. Suffice it to say, the other brothers might frown upon him inviting a couple who embody two abominations over for tea at the monastery. If it were only me, well, I'm his daughter and very few monks have kids, so they'll make an exception. But bringing in visible evidence of my *practicing* homosexuality wouldn't do at all. (The pope actually said it was OK to be homosexual as long as you weren't "practicing," to which I replied, "No problem, I've got it down.")

Back to Mom—she's much more fun. One year my mother took me aside and very seriously said, "I'm trying to understand this whole gay thing, and what I don't get—I mean, when a man's with a man and a woman's with a woman—how do you know who's who?" I was speechless. I finally replied, "We introduce ourselves?" Was my mother asking me if I was a top or bottom, butch or femme? There are places that parents and their children shouldn't go. This is one of them. Mom, lay off the eggnog. This sort of parent will also ask that you keep it to the immediate family that the woman you brought home is your lover. The Jerry Springer–type parent fears a domino-like effect of heart attacks for all family members over 65 if they were to realize that Connie is not your roommate but your lover. The fatalities would be instantaneous. Underlying this request is the belief that being gay could be a phase, so why upset the older ones? Right, a phase. And the family turkey, dressing and all, will get up and recite some Walt Whitman, followed by a tribute to k.d. lang. Not in this girl's lifetime.

Family. All that therapy and still the struggle continues. For some of us, the family warms up pretty quickly; for the majority, it takes some time and effort; and still for others, the possibility of acceptance is close to futile. It's very sad for that last group, but that's why so many of us have our gay families too.

Testing the Waters: Your First Vacation Together

The real test of any romance is traveling together. First off, assume there will be a big pre-trip fight. This is normal. In fact, the longer you've been together the more vicious the fight. It'll be about packing, being late for the plane, or who forgot the sunblock. Not to worry: Once you're actually on the plane or all packed up and on the road, you'll remember she's your sweetie even if you were right.

I'm convinced that couples get together based on one being the meticulous planner type and one being more of a last-minute wing-it type. I had one GF who was *so* meticulous that on a cross-country road trip she had not only gone to AAA and plotted the entire route but highlighted the rest stops. I found that to be very impressive, since I'm more the "toss a few T-shirts and hair products in a bag and go" type.

In the long run, these differences are a good thing. It's when they're so glaring and annoying that it's important to be patient with your lover. Patient, patient, patient.

The best example I have of a great and disastrous vacation within a long-term relationship is the time my ex Isabelle and I went to Paris. Yes, Paris,the city d'amour—that is, once you get over the jet lag, the money changing, and taking the adventure-filled high-speed train and Metro from the airport to your hotel. Once all that's done, what a city! Especially in autumn: The tourist crowds are virtually nonexistent, but it's still bustling though not rushed. The leaves on all the trees appear in hues of gold, red, green, and orange, letting you know where Monet and his impressionist buddies got their ideas.

One of the reasons we had chosen Paris in October is that I was serving as a guest director at the Paris Lesbian Film Festival, where we would have free accommodations for three nights. Finally, some fringe benefits as an independent filmmaker! And to have a girlfriend who spoke fluent French and had dual citizenship—it was too perfect. I, on the other hand, have my two-semester French speaking style that has me saying things like "You are a cigarette" rather than "You don't smoke?" But the French were exceptionally kind and forgiving of my odd usage, contrary to popular myth.

My girlfriend was less than sympathetic to my constant, *"Comment c'est dit 'luggage'?"* Tip: When going to a foreign country with a lover who speaks the native language fluently, have a little sit-down prior to departure. Discuss, oh, how much translating you'll want or need and what style of vacation you each are imagining. My girlfriend and I apparently were on two totally different vacations for most of the trip. I was happy to be going to a beautiful Parisian spot, walking, walking, walking, then sitting in a café, watching, listening, and drinking really strong coffee.

Isabelle wanted to show me everything in the city she knows so well. In one week. In a city that has more museums, monuments, history, churches, and some of the most elaborate architecture in Western civilization. Simply put: Compromise is good for your sex life.

Before leaving for Paris we did our homework—I bought a guidebook called *Cheap Eats in Paris* (you can see my expectations are lofty), and my girlfriend picked up *Gay Paris*. Since Paris doesn't have a truly "gay" neighborhood, I was impressed by how they stretched the topic out into an entire book (maps take up a lot of space).

Isabelle and I did locate a reasonable and comfortable hotel through this book. Not only did we get fresh croissants and café au lait in the morning, but there was a sweet cat who accepted affection from everybody. This is not at all odd in a town that allows one's dogs on the Metro and in many restaurants. The Parisians sure love their dogs, especially the small fluffy kind.

The closest Paris has to a gay area is in an older, quite beautiful *arrondissement* called Le Marais. It's a sort of "after work" gay central. Queers don't necessarily live there, but there are many queer or queer-friendly bars, restaurants, and hotels. One feels safe and welcomed holding hands, kissing, and generally being gay-gay-gay-gay-gay.

This is not the case in the rest of Paris. I was surprised that when my girlfriend and I held hands while walking along the Seine, we were stared at quite blatantly and disapprovingly. Once, when we kissed, I saw a 50-something couple literally stop in their tracks (à la Wile E. Coyote). I felt like screaming, *Get a life! This is Paris—don't you know how sophisticated and intellectual you're supposed to be!* It wasn't horrible, but it wasn't San Francisco either.

Back to Le Marais. We were shopping for a restaurant when we came upon Le Gai Moulin. As we read the menu outside, the waiter (who turned out to be the owner) waved us in with such an engaging a smile that we bite. Le Gai Moulin manages to fit more people in per square queer inch than the Metro at rush hour. The tables are tiny, and you can't help but be friendly to those dining next to you. One false move and someone's *poisson provençal* might become airborne.

But what the restaurant lacked in culinary greatness, it more than made up for in festive atmosphere. We traded jokes with our neighbors as the owner entertained everyone in both French and English. He clearly was a man who truly loved his work. And we truly loved dining with him.

The Paris Lesbian Film Festival was held at a very arty, oh-so-French theater. A glass pyramid structure fronts the building and is a walkway to the Grande Salle (big theater). On the downside, the festival is held in Montreuil, which, though technically in Paris, is like going to a San Francisco film festival held in Daly City or a New York City festival in the Bronx.

Talk about cultural differences. Looking for lunch, my girlfriend and I went to the neighborhood bistro. I thought it a great idea, as I'd get a glimpse of what "real" French people do—what they eat, where they hang out, and the general atmosphere of a more working-class establishment.

Near our table stood a man playing a pinball machine. He was an older gentleman and immediately took a liking to me—I mean, really took a liking to me. I hadn't been so objectified since the '80s. Apparently, the way he decided to get my attention was by expelling the most enormous streams of foul-smelling smoke in my direction. I literally couldn't breathe. I changed my seat. This did not deter him. My girlfriend said it was a cultural thing. Now, I'm all for cultural enlightenment, but I draw the line at death by slimy-guy secondhand smoke.

Interestingly, he clearly had no clue we were gay girls, as were the women at the next table over. Considering the festival's proximity and what had to be an increase in lesbian business, the man might have caught on. Our "sporty" American attire tricked him, I guess. Did this guy really think he had a chance? Did his smoky pickup trick ever work with any woman?

The senior citizen women seated behind us, however, weren't fooled for a minute. They threw us nasty looks at every opportunity. My girlfriend said it was because we were on their turf and that they probably hated Americans, not lesbians. That was somehow comforting. Kind of nice to be hated for something else for a change.

Back to the festival and French bureaucracy: As in all lesbian-nation events worldwide, there were numerous ambiguous lines to be waited in. It was a rather elaborate setup. First, you had to buy whatever number of tickets you wanted. Then the day of the chosen film, again, you had to queue up to get the actual ticket for the screening. Being a director, I was permitted to skip the first step but not the second.

Parisian lesbians definitely exhibited a wide range of haircuts and had a penchant for bright colors—especially orange. I'm not sure why. Couples over 40 tended to be look-alike "identi-dykes," as in the States. Festivalgoers under 40 sported a variety of looks. One noticeable thing: The butch/femme presence was very low to nonexistent. Maybe it hasn't quite hit the other side of the Atlantic yet.

My two comic videos did fine, considering the obstacles. Unfortunately, reading English subtitles and missing half the images while doing so certainly hurt the laughter quotient. And my pristine Beta tapes (one-inch broadcast quality) didn't play well on the equipment. One tape pitched everyone's voice an octave lower—which was fine for some of the characters, but unfortunately I was in one video and have a very low voice to begin with. Result? I sounded beyond demonic. My VHS preview copies were used instead and came out in black-and-white (I'd shot the videos in color). Basically, it was a disaster, but people still laughed—well, some did, and at odd places.

Still, I recommend Paris in the fall to anyone, regardless of whether there's going to be another lesbian film festival. It's an amazing and truly romantic city. It can be a great place to have that first "we're a couple" vacation, especially if you get all the petty arguments out of the way during that *long* 11-hour plane flight.

And just getting to your hotel together may bond you two in a whole new way.

Polyamory
(Or, When One Is Not Enough)

Polyamory: I looked up the term in my huge, industrial-strength Webster's dictionary. It's not in there, though *poly* is, and it means "an element meaning 'much' or 'many.' " *Amory* isn't in there either, but *amor* is and has a one-word definition: Cupid. So taken all together it means "many Cupids." I sort of like that. Who wouldn't want many Cupids in their lives? It sounds so full of endless possibilities. This is a good thing in matters of the heart.

A friend of mine who's heavily into polyamory explains, "It takes a lot of pressure off the relationship. When a monogamous relationship fails, you're alone. If you have several relationships to begin with, getting out of one that doesn't work out isn't quite as traumatic." She makes a good point. But I'm compelled to play devil's advocate here by citing my own experience: The more deeply in love you are, the more painful the breakup—and the same holds true for many of my friends, both male and female. Looked at in another way, if you've had one foot out of the water all along, it's not that hard to pull out the other foot. But who's to say you can't have both feet in the water with more than one person? Would this require additional limbs?

Consider also the possibility that the feet, limbs and waters intersect, à la ménage à trois (or quatre, etc.)—similar to the Venn diagram we learned in junior high. For those who

171

can't quite remember, it was three distinct circles that over-lapped with one another in a triangular configuration. It was used to illustrate sets, subsets, and their relationships (again, Webster's definition). Roughly that translates to: At some point everyone sleeps with everyone else in couples or trios. I'm exhausted just thinking about the possibilities. A inter-sects with B creating AB; B intersects C creating BC, A inter-sects with C creating AC; A,B, and C intersect creating ABC, or should they all get a new letter all together?

In a perfect world, I believe that polyamory could work for me. But sadly the one time I dated and slept with two different women at the same time within a month, both women dumped me. I was totally on the up and up about it. I told them about each other right away—not in detail, of course. Oddly, they both asked me out in the same calendar week and I didn't know either of them very well. But it was easy to tell them apart: One was adding to her Anne Klein collection and the other was adding to her tattoos. So I briefly mentioned to each of them that I was also seeing someone else—was that OK? It was, apparently, until I actually slept with both of them and showed no signs of ditching one for the other. I liked them both, and I'd never been so popular. I asked a therapist friend, Nan, if this was weird. She didn't think so. But apparently they sure as hell did.

I decided to do some additional research on this, so I called my gay boyfriend Jim. He's done it all…twice. During his experiences with being polyamorous, he always ended up liking one guy more than the other. When he was with the "less-liked" guy, he'd end up feeling guilty. And I quote Jim:

"What was I supposed to say, 'I like you less, but the other guy's not available, so you'll do?' "

In another ménage à trois, where all three had sex both separately as couples and as a trio (draw the Venn diagram, do the math, and get back to me), Jim apparently ended up as the "mistress guy." Eventually, the other two got together as a couple, and he became the occasional plaything. In the spirit of "We're not like straight people; so what if I'm the mistress...the mistress can be special too!" he carried on in this capacity for a few more months. Then he realized in fact that his feelings were hurt, and he didn't want to be the "special mistress guy"; he wanted to be the "special boyfriend/lover."

One of the neurotic problems I have with participating in polyamory is that I already have a pathological fear that I will call a newish lover by the wrong name. Which makes no sense since it has never happened. And this is not necessarily in the throes of passion—it could be while asking her pass the salt. In a poly situation my fear would be doubled or tripled. Then there are the time constraints. I can spend an hour picking out a card for the object of my lust/affection. Multiply by three and there goes the day job. Not that I have a day job, but if I did, I would cease to have time for it.

The majority of the polyamorous people I've known whose situation lasted more than six months have been either bisexual, or there's a primary committed relationship with one or both partners having a steady lover outside of the relationship. One polyamorous woman I know had four lovers total: two men and two women. She actually had to draw a diagram for me to illustrate who slept with whom. It started to resemble something from molecular science. Two of the men and one of the women and herself all cohabited and were in a committed household for more than three years. She also had a female lover outside of the primary four lovers. They had very strict rules regarding safe sex, and if you wanted to add someone new to your life, you had to get the group's approval. Now, this didn't mean that anyone else in the stable ongoing foursome would or could have relations with the new person. It was more that it was important to everyone that there was some level of trust.

Think about it: Four people who cohabit and sleep together in varying couples may also have a lover or two outside of the primary committed group. I swear this is true. This woman said they had a schedule designating who slept with whom each night. I am not making this up. Interestingly, all the women were bisexual, and none of the men were. Kinsey proven right again: Men are rigid and consistent in their sexual object choices; women are fluid and flexible. I asked my friend about the jealousy factor, and yes, it did happen, but you had to work it out for yourself. It was in very bad form to act out your jealousy. She said this aspect actually made for learning greater autonomy. I found this amazing. I had to ask about the time constraints/exhaustion factor. She said that definitely was an issue. You had to be very sure you were willing to put in the time, and it *did* take up a lot of time. To her, however, it was well worth it. I was and remain impressed that they could pull this off.

If I imagine myself in such a scenario, I'm the problem

child. I overanalyze all things libidinous as it is. It wouldn't be four times more time analyzing—it would be exponential (back to the Venn diagram). Then there's the implicit emotional generosity. I simply don't think I could be in love with, or a loving partner to, that many people.

I think polyamory can and does work for some people. I just don't think I'm one of them, possibly because I already have three careers and have a hard enough time dating one person, let alone a group. Unless they're a world-class basketball or soccer team, in which case I'd make an exception. After all, they'd be on the road a lot and there'd be *so* many to chose from. OK, a girl can dream.

When Your Friend's Spouse Is Beyond a Drag

This is an issue suggested by my big sister—heterosexual, lest you think my parents were two for two in the gay-girl category. One of her larger problems regarding friendships is the Spousal Unit who's a major drag. We *all* know this one, no matter how your sexuality expresses itself. It goes like this: Remember your good friend? The one you laughed with until you cried, ate brownies out of the pan with, and generally had a blast with? That is, until *she* came along—the *she* being a Spousal Unit who subtly but effectively destroys any social engagement. Unbelievably, your friend—no chimp, she—does not have a clue, an inkling, or even a coherent thought about this. What the hell happened? It's almost like your once lively, delightful friend has had a lobotomy, a personality transplant, an invasion of the body snatchers.

What to do? If you want to stay friends, unless you think your friend is in danger of bodily harm, no matter how obnoxious, controlling or plain-out weird you may find a friend's choice in dating, you never, *ever* say what you really think until way after the breakup. And I mean *way* after. Not that very week or even the next, because, as experience tells us, they could get back together. No, more like a month down the road when for sure you know she's never going back with her/him. Most people learn this the hard way by the time they leave high school.

These are treacherous waters, as many women who have tried to subtly or not so subtly point out a friend's girlfriend's flaws have discovered. The expression "love is blind" is never truer than in these situations. How, you ask yourself repeatedly, does your friend not see this? For example, let's say you and your friend have a standing date to see any new Ben Stiller movie. You call to firm up the plan on Monday, as it opens Friday. Friday afternoon your friend calls and leaves a message for you at home, when she knows your work number, so it's extra lame, with some excuse like "Barb's great-aunt is in town. Maybe next week? Oh, that's not actually good either—we're going on this retreat thing. I'll call you." "WHAT?!" you not so graciously scream at your answering machine. "We're talking Ben Stiller here, and she thinks I can wait three weeks?" For that matter, what's happened that now *she* can wait three weeks?

To be clear, I am not referring to the honeymoon phase that we all give our friends lots of slide on. This is different. This is many months into the relationship, and we're talking about a years-old tradition. Don't tell me she's robbed you of loving all things Ben Stiller? That is simply going too far.

Before you know it, it's become a given that the time you do spend with your friend includes said Unit (as you fondly think of her). This transition happens very slyly. Example: You ask your friend if she wants to shoot hoops, and you hear a muffled, "Honey, want to go to the park with Mo and play some basketball?" More muffled sounds. "Sure. We'll meet you around 2." Wait a second—how can three people play one-on-one? And who said anything about 2 P.M.? Who invited *her*? I didn't hear myself say, "How 'bout you and Unit and I shoot some hoops?" God forbid *my friend* has a laugh or two with someone who is not *she*.

Soon you'll notice that if you want to see your friend at all—or ever again—you're the one who has to make the plans, make the call, etc., which feels unreciprocal. In fact, you're starting to feel downright insulted. At the beginning all the blame is heaped upon Unit. Then it dawns on you: It takes two. You're friend has become a wimp, a mutant of her former self. How could this happen? When you do spend time with the two of them, you notice she takes all her cues from Unit. For instance, after a seeing a play together, you ask, "How about getting some tapas?" She looks over at Unit who gives her the not so secret signal *no*. You cringe at seeing the non-verbal exchange, which also translates as, *Activity only, no chatty-time.*

If you're single, all of this is worse. The two of them will start socializing with other couples only. Given their example, you don't feel especially inspired to go out and find the woman of your dreams. So that will further dwindle the amount of time you spend with your friend. You know she's in there somewhere. But where and when will she reappear, if ever?

If you're in a relationship, given that Unit is on the scene, the assumption is that you'll double-date, no matter how dull or mismatched the grouping is. Your lover will resent these outings. Chances are, she'll feel the same as you about Unit: a cross between loathing and morbid fascination. She'll have the good sense to have a migraine the next time there's a double date. Your lover will also miss the old version of your friend and wisely advise you to tell her point blank that you and Unit have no rapport, could you do things just with each other again?

This could make or break the friendship. If she's gone to the dark side—by that, I mean she's changed so much that she defends her lover—you're dead in the water. If there's a remnant of the old friend, she may think over whether she should socialize alone with you and decide it's a good idea, though she knows it will mean a battle with Unit. This may lead to her questioning why Unit is so protective of her time. Or your friend may give it a shot, and Unit will make her so miserable before or after the outing that either she'll decide it's not worth it (she shows up in a foul mood, anyway) or they'll have a blowout of a fight. The latter could actually work in your favor as your friend's old personality makes a comeback, rising out of the pheromonal/family scripts/psychobabble quagmire of her relationship with Unit. She'll see what has been obvious to you all along: that if you wake up one morning to find that there's barely a shred of your real personality, you are with the wrong person. Compromise is one thing, co-opting another.

Sadly, you may have lost your friend for the duration of her relationship with Unit—a duration you can only pray is short. Or the relationship will go on so long that you lose your friend forever because even if years later she has disposed of Unit, your feelings will have been so hurt that there's no going back. Now, *that's* truly a drag.

Should We or Shouldn't We Move In?

If I weren't so squirrelly about my privacy and tangible-type commitment, this might actually be fun. Think about it: You love each other, get to sleep together every night, split gas and electric bills—what could be bad? The optimistic, in-love part of me is all for it. The neurotic "Oh, God, you can't get away—help!" part of me just completely rearranged the living room furniture, sorted four bags worth of recycling, and mink-oiled a pair of boots I haven't worn since 1991—all so I could avoid writing this chapter. And I don't even know what mink oil is.

What happens if she moves everything in and the dreaded LBD (Lesbian Bed Death) sets in? One thing that should not be tolerated in a relationship is going for months without sex. All that communicating clearly and compromising and you're not even indulging in the joy of gay-girl she-love? I don't think so. Suppose she has odd habits she's successfully hidden from me—like flossing her teeth in the living room? Suppose her chow/husky dog eats one of my kitties? Suppose she folds her towels in quarters instead of thirds? I know, I know, this is important stuff.

Then there are all the "whose furniture?" and "whose kitchenware?" decisions. Most important: the bed. One must go in storage. At this point, there are readers all over the country (except in Manhattan and San Francisco) who are thinking: Why not just get a two-bedroom apartment? Because this is San Francisco, which has a 0% vacancy rate. Someone puts a FOR RENT sign in a window, and it's worse than a Grateful Dead concert. People camp out for days, hoping to be among the first 40 applicants to look at the place. And don't even get me started on the rents.

Back to beds. Will it be my yummy Posturepedic full-size bed (with my 10 sets of fabulous sheets, a minor obsession) or her queen/king or whatever size bed? I clearly prefer...*my* bed. I do have an advantage: I have two bad discs. I could play the bad-back card. Even though it's absolutely true, I'd feel guilty anyway.

Then there's the whole money thing. When and do you get a joint checking account, or keep the money separate? I hate couples that are so autonomous they pay separately at restaurants. This is taking it too far. I don't even like to date that way. At least take turns and assume it all comes out close to even anyway. I say no joint checking account until you've cohabited for at least a year. That way, if she has a secret retail therapy addiction, you won't get stuck paying off those creditors since she fled to parts unknown. Trust: It's all about trust. Of which I have little, apparently.

I say all this fully knowing that I gave one girlfriend—of the two live-in lovers I've had—a credit card for her use, since it was so expensive to move to San Francisco. I did have her name put on the card along with mine, however, which turned out to be a good move. That was eight years ago, and I haven't seen her in six. I don't know what happened to that card. But I assume she still has it or burned it, because no one's ever asked me to pay up. So even after a crappy breakup, she's done the honorable thing, but I also thought we were "till death do us part." At least I thought so that first year. My sister says that money is one of the hardest things to deal with in a relationship, so you've got to pick and choose your battles and let the rest of it go.

Then there's noise level. *Huh?* you may be thinking. Clearly, noise is one of my pet peeves. I am greatly annoyed and distracted by loud televisions, radios, or music. I love music—just not cranked up so that the walls vibrate. I'm such a delicate flower. I seem to attract droves of women with incredibly high thresholds to sound. Thank the goddess for headphones. Even I love them. And I'm sure they've saved more than one relationship. Your lover's predilection for noise, however, should have been apparent before you moved in together. Many people, though, are on their Sunday-best compromise behavior when living apart. Once you've inadvertently witnessed any one of numerous and unattractive bodily functions emanating from your lover, things tend to change. This includes things like volume level, money, who did the dishes last, and why you got so little room in the main clothes closet.

The bottom line for me is that I'm wary of the "this is it forever" part. I'm either too realistic, too cynical, or too emotionally twisted for that. Living together is a *big deal* for several reasons: (1) We are talking major commitment; (2) I enjoy my solitude—of which I get plenty; and (3) you *can't* get away! I know I don't sound overly mature or even moderately mature. I know that when the topic comes up again, I'll probably be so in love that all of this will be negligible. I'll throw all caution—well, most caution—to the wind. There will always be a part of my psyche that equates mate-like living situations with prison. And this is contrary to the two experiences I've had. Go figure.

For all the aforementioned drawbacks to living together, there *is* the upside. Coming home after an especially rough day to find your lover has whipped up a great meal and offers you a yummy neck massage does have its advantages. Cuddling up to that familiar warmth and smell of your sleeping lover when a nightmare wakes you up can work like a sleep potion—a pleasant alternative to, as in years gone by, getting up alone at 3 A.M. and pacing and wondering about *everything* you did wrong in your entire life, apparently the only topic available after 2 A.M. Instead, you'll be warm and safe and pretty sure you've done one good thing. And she's sleeping right next to you.

Mo's Commitment Ceremony Do's and Don'ts

For those determined to go all the way and have a commitment ceremony/marriage, here's a helpful list of don'ts I've accrued from my own and other's experiences with these events. I mean this in the kindest possible way, my sister-woman-sister. I'm 100% percent behind the idea that gay-girl commitment ceremonies don't or shouldn't have to mimic their heterosexual counterparts. But this is not an excuse to leap with abandon into the tacky, the embarrassing (for guests), or a lack of preparation.

• Don't have a potluck—even if you're broke. That's what credit cards are for. Or have a small tasteful gathering the two of you can afford.

• Don't enter your bridal registry at Home Depot. Too much practically can set a less-than-romantic tone.

• Don't make everyone else do positive affirmations or crystal touching of any sort. You don't want to make your less than New Age friends/relatives uncomfortable. (At the very least make it optional, with a stocked bar and hors d'oeuvres ready for those who don't wish to participate.)

• Don't wear the same outfit—i.e., matching dresses or tuxes. It's plain-out weird. Be autonomous individuals. Coordinating bouquets/boutonnieres, however, is fine. Say it with flowers, not creepy Freudian doppelgänger outfits.

- Don't have either of your exes, no matter how close a friend she now is, perform the ceremony. Again, just too damn weird.

- Don't invite hostile relatives. It is, after all, your day. Surround yourself with true loved ones.

- Do make it clear to your guests that this is a dressy affair. One wouldn't wear jeans at their siblings' wedding—why should this be any different?

- Do make sure there are more than enough refreshments. Don't count on a deity changing your water into wine.

- Do have the time of your life, and your guests will follow suit.

Baby Maybe?

Babies. Beautiful bundles of untarnished perfection—except for all that unfortunate leaking. When they're scrubbed and cooing, they melt all my reservations. How can I not want one of my own? Then I think of all that responsibility and I sink like a stone.

When I ponder how I was raised, it's amazing I survived my childhood at all. My mother was overwhelmed, bearing four children in just four-and-a-half years. I'm not kidding. Things were different then: There were no milk-carton missing children, no baby seats, no bike helmets. All summer long Mom would send us out on our bikes, in Philadelphia, from morning to dinnertime with nary a thought. We'd have white-bread peanut butter and grape jelly sandwiches slipped into plastic baggies and off we'd go. In the heat and humidity, lunch became more of a casserole than a sandwich by the time we got to it. When I was in second grade, the youngest of us, my baby brother, was only 5. We'd go to the rec center; we'd play on the swings and monkey bars, swim, and join any team that would have us. All day long. We were more or less forbidden to venture home before dinner unless violent weather or emergency room level injuries had occurred.

Swimming was my favorite. Since there were too many kids for the pool to accommodate at one time, the play schedule was broken down by sex: Mondays, Wednesdays, Fridays were "girls" days; Tuesdays, Thursdays, and Saturdays were "boys" days. I always resented that the boys got Saturdays, because they'd get an entire day during the week to swim before school let out and the schedule changed. Sunday was "Family Day," and you weren't let in without an adult. So, of course, since our parents rarely, if ever went, we'd join other families. The four little Brownsey kids joining the eight Mangatelli kids. There was something sweet in this casual relationship. Adults screamed and yelled at will. It didn't matter that they weren't your parents—they could still yell at you.

And we weren't alone. It was a style of parenting. What were these people thinking? I'm not complaining—we all survived, but I'm still amazed that we did. The older kids minded the littler kids; it was a Darwinian *Lord of the Flies* situation. Sometimes it wasn't pretty. Some of them were nice; some were preparing for a future in slumlording.

Why this trip down memory lane? Because I think it has a direct impact on my fear of having children of my own. Not that I'd send them out in the inner city on a bike once they turned 5. On the contrary, I think I'd be wildly overprotective and scared for their safety 24/7. This fear is compounded by the expensive and nerve-racking artificial-insemination aspect of being a lesbian mom. I know it's worth it—every lesbian mom I know is thrilled with her offspring. But it's so much commitment month in and month out, and then there's all that waiting. I guess it's like that for all parents-to-be—the waiting part anyway.

Then there's the incredible amount of red tape and terror for the nonbirth mom to adopt the child legally. I've seen several friends endure that process, and even in San Francisco it's a nightmare. I can imagine that it's far more difficult—or even impossible—in other parts of the country.

All of this, for me anyway, is contingent upon my having a life partner, which has not been my strong suit. I don't think it has anything to do with my being a *très* gay girl (I'm surrounded by long-term lesbian couples); I think it's sort of the luck of the draw. Who knows? My two previous attempts at "life partnering" ended after three-and-a-half and two years respectively. Longer than the average life of a fruit fly, shorter than that of a parakeet. I'd like to move into the mammal life span at the very least before considering having my own genetically linked mammal.

Now, the big plus to mom-mom parenting: If the women are both between, say, 18 and 40, generally either one of them could be the birth mother. For some couples, both women are so anxious to have a child that they race to the sperm bank, basal thermometer in hand, yelling, "No, me first, *me*!" Others have the opposite problem: They want a child, but neither wants to actually go through pregnancy and childbirth. I know one couple who went back and forth about this for a year. A typical conversation ran along these lines:

"But you have better genes—my grandfather has diabetes."

"Diabetes skips a generation—you're the one at risk."

"Exactly. Plus you'd make a cuter baby—you have the prettiest eyes."

"And the donor might have squinty eyes or some recessive gene might pop up that neither of us has. Besides, your whole family lives forever. You're the only person I know over the age of 30 with all four of her grandparents still alive."

"So, they live longer—I could drop dead of diabetes any day."

(It is at about this point that logic and scientific fact are freely tossed out.)

"And I have a bad back. Could you see me with all that extra weight in the front? They'd have to hang weights over my shoulder to counterbalance me so I wouldn't be in traction the last four months."

"Please, you strained your back picking up a picnic table to impress me."

"Fine. We'll adopt."

"No way—with our great gene pools we'd be crazy to adopt."

"Then you and your gene pool can have the baby. I'll open doors for you and get you ice cream at 3 A.M."

"No way. I've seen too many TV births where the women are writhing in the agony of the damned. Now, *that's* pain."

"Make them give you drugs. I would."

"See, you already know what you'd do…."

Finally, the couple decided to take turns inseminating. Miss "I might drop dead from diabetes" went first and of course got pregnant immediately. Interestingly, after the morning sickness wore off, she got really into it. And against the odds she had a girl.

Which brings us to the question, why do so many lesbians have boys? The rate has got to be 90%. It's been explained to me several times, and I can never quite get it. With that caveat,

I believe it has something to do with the XY chromosomes swimming to the top of the place they keep the sperm while it's waiting. I imagine teardrop-shaped sperm, with little faces, playing poker, killing time, smoking cigars, drinking beer, and not letting any of the XX's in the game. Something about cylindrical force... (More "Mo-science.") Anyway, they're all having boys. This will make for some interesting coming-of-age movies in about 20 years; charming, wack period pieces about growing up with two moms at the dawn of the new millennium.

One issue that cannot go unmentioned is when a couple will start having sex after birthing. Knowing several lesbian moms, I know for a fact that it's anywhere from six months to two years, depending on their exhaustion level. Projectile vomiting is not exactly an aphrodisiac. Going more than two months without sleeping for more than three hours in a row can lead to psychosis, let alone dim the libido. Bluntly put, babies are work. Hard work. Constant work. Even though everyone with a baby always follows up a very legitimate baby complaint with the phrase, "But it's so worth it—just look at him/her."

Back to sex: I'd pray big time to get a "sleeper," an infant who sleeps through the night after the first couple weeks of life so that my partner and I might revive our sex life. It can happen—my sister got a sleeper. Of course, that could reduce my odds of having one: I think only one sleeper per family is allowed. Though I don't think the sleep factor would be a major reason for or against having sex. On second thought, I can be a real bitch when exhausted. No child should have to put up with that.

Another issue that cannot go unaddressed is what if you *don't* want to have a baby? My friend Sheila has never had one molecule of maternal baby-from-my-body lust. On more than one occasion, she's copped to that fact in public, and the other lesbians on hand have looked at her as if she'd just emitted some foul odor. Sheila also does not have a shy proton in her body and will step right up and defend her point of view: "So? What's your problem? I have a womb. Therefore, if I don't use it, am I a cruel, unfeeling person? Does it mean I'll lead an empty and pathetic existence, eventually throwing myself off a cliff in babyless despair? *What?*" Most moms or moms-to-be will try to get out of it gracefully, because (a) Sheila is right, and (b) she will take anyone on toe-to-toe until she wins—which she always does. Personally, I find the extreme pro-baby attitude very odd, given how many gay girls are feminist and pro-choice. So, if you're one of the above, lighten up. The world's overpopulated as it is anyway. Sheesh.

In the end, I have to admit that I'm intrigued with this whole parent thing. I still have time, though at this point my eggs are numbered. I just reassure myself that one of the coolest things about being a gay girl is that your girlfriend can have the baby.

part six

The (Gulp) Breakup

- how to actually do it and mean it
- when ignorance is NOT bliss
- screaming red flags that it is O-V-E-R

How to Break Up the Gay-Girl Relationship: A Start-up Kit

One unique aspect to gay-girl dating is the frequency of breakups that start in one fashion era and conclude in another. What's the holdup, ladies? You don't need to prove the myth that a lesbian breakup lasts at least half as long as the relationship itself. Yes, it's hard—that's why they call it a *break*up, not "two autonomous people going their separate ways." But it does not have to go on, year in and year out. This is completely needless torture. To assist you through the breakup process, I've devised the following guide so you can pick up the pace and create what I refer to as a "quick death."

Step 1: I Say Libido, You Say Lobotomy

Begin with endless fights in which one or both women claim the other isn't listening and is *so* self-centered. You can follow this up with arguments about money, her omnipresent best friend who is also her ex, and the fact that you only have sex when *she* wants to. "She" is interchangeable for both parties, since in a pinch either can claim that she was the first to initiate. "Why do you think I shaved my legs?!!" That you shave daily won't matter in the heat of the argument, unless she's a lawyer by trade, in which case she'll always fight better, even when she's wrong. If this is the case, skip to Step 3.

Step 2: It's Not Me, It's You!

At this point you've both identified that you have "issues" as a couple. You will go back and forth on this until one of you suggests couples counseling. The other will probably resist, offering the "It's not that bad—we can work it out on our own" argument. Believe me, once the phrase "couples counseling" escapes someone's lips, there are only two options left in your relationship: (a) you're going, or (b) it's over. Now, if you've been together six months or less, get out! Of course, since 95% of all lesbians hate the cold, cruel dating world, most will do anything to prolong a relationship. Therefore, proceed to step 3.

Step 3: Couples Counseling, or She Said/She Said

A truly thorough and pragmatic couple will actually shop for a therapist. This is because a "biased" therapist can encourage even more fighting ("She likes you more than me." Or, "I can't believe I'm paying $100 an hour to have you nurtured by a stranger because you cry more easily than I do!") At the beginning, counseling will bolster the couple's bond, since they're taking a proactive stance. This fades by session 2, when they find out they do in fact have to do "the work." It's at this point that some relationships get back on track. But for the doomed, therapy is basically a money pit that teaches you new terminology that you can use in your next relationship; for example, "When you say X, it brings up my Y issues. If you try to avoid the phrase X, I will try not to connect you with trauma Y. Therapy can go on for six months to 10 years, depending on laziness, tenacity, and the couple's joint property holdings.

Step 4: Breaking Up (Really)

This is when you calmly and tearfully decide it's over. The problem here is that almost all lesbians cohabit, so someone will have to move out. The moving-out process can last from one month (healthy) to three years (twisted). I've known lesbians so stubborn that they continued to live together for years until one them finally fell in love with someone else. At this point the other woman will be furious and either move out in a huff or change the locks. My strong advice (not that you asked): When it's over, get out! Screw the money and inconvenience. Toss a coin to see who gets the apartment and get on it with your life. Even if you do this, it may not prevent step 5.

Step 5: I Can't Believe I Slept With Her Again!

This can happen after it's over and you've moved out, but you both decide to stay friends. In that spirit, you have her over for dinner. You laugh together; you remember why you fell in love with her originally. Then you sleep with her, have the best sex you've had in years, and wake up back in the relationship. And then you remember your breakup started two years ago in couples counseling. This repeat phase can last one night (if you're lucky) or an additional number of years with another move-in and move-out.

◆ ◆ ◆

I'm not sure about this, but maybe the only way to get out of a lesbian relationship quickly and cleanly is if one person does something so despicable (lie, cheat, steal) that there's absolutely no going back. These are by far the best breakups. Even though the pain is excruciating for the offended party, it is a clear and righteous pain with a swift conclusion.

The Seven Deadly Causes of Breakups

Of all the things that can go wrong in a relationship, it occurred to me to see how they related to the seven deadly sins. Those would be jealousy, sloth, vanity, greed, pride, lust, and deceit. Some permutation of one of these is generally at the center of the breakup. Fortunately, if one of these characteristics is obvious early on, you'll know better than to even get into a long-term relationship. I'll start with my least favorite:

Jealousy

First, I have to admit I have a rather one-sided relationship with jealousy. I don't get jealous; I just get out. My logic: You want her, fine. Don't let the door hit your butt on the way out. Then, in the next few days, I will eat one box or six of Froot Loops (depending on my level of heartbreak). After a few days of consuming nothing but sugar, coupled with the side effect that the roof of my mouth has shed several layers of post-Loops skin, I'll begin phoning my friends. They'll all assure me she's an idiot to have cheated on me and dumped me for another; clearly, she has no sense of personal ethics. Each of these assurances will make me feel better for about an hour. Fortunately, I have enough friends that eventually I'll believe someone. This is what friends are for, so save your therapy money for the really big problems.

From watching people I've known over the years—gay, bi, trans, or straight—I've learned that jealousy is a common human trait. I've seen my share of drinks thrown by one gay man into another man's face for blatantly cruising. Ditto heterosexuals, though that mostly happens in movies.

Now the Catholic schoolgirl in me must add that jealousy is one of the seven deadly sins. It's up there with lust and greed—all *active* cardinal sins. Sloth is gross but generally doesn't cause you to fantasize revenge of the tire-slashing, death, and humiliation magnitude. Unless of course you're living with a sloth, in which case all bets are off. Someone who consistently thinks all floors are very flat laundry baskets can inspire all kinds resentments turned evil.

For whatever reason, a pronounced tendency toward jealousy is a prerequisite for anyone who wants to date me—casually or seriously. I'm not sure whether most gay girls are jealous in greater numbers or if I just attract them. Odd, considering that I've met a lot of my girlfriends/affairs/lovers on the road or through comedy. I didn't know they were jealous at the beginning because lust (another one of the big 7) essentially blinds me for the first few weeks to small details, such as *the* one character trait that is a completely unsuitable in a road comic's lover.

What I mean is this: Why would someone who knows herself to be the jealous type even consider dating someone who's the focal point of throngs of gay girls? Someone who makes them laugh, then goes back to her hotel room by herself with no one to talk to? It's like a diabetic dating a sugar addict. Why torture yourself?

I've never quite grasped jealousy. What's the point? If she's going to go off with some other babe, what can I do anyway? If we're in a monogamous relationship, I assume that means she won't be sleeping with someone else. If she does, it's never occurred to me to hate the other woman, want to be her, displace her, whatever. She's not the one I've just been trashed by. Unless she's a friend (now former friend) and that's another scenario all together. That's down there in the scum category, and I think you can safely fantasize particularly gruesome outcomes for the new couple with impunity.

Lest I sound like a paragon of mental health and confidence, rest assured that I've had more than my share of "Why do I feel like a geeky 12-year-old again?" moments of wanting to leap out of the car, dash out of the restaurant, and never pick up the phone again. Dating can make me that nervous. I just don't quite get the jealousy thing. Actually I do get it, but only by proxy.

Sloth

Sloth is one of the seven deadly sins that few will admit to since it's so unattractive. I've dated a lot of women who freely admit that they are the jealous type. And people frequently confess that their pride or vanity "got in the way." But you hardly ever hear someone say, "My sloth is hurting my relationship." Granted, it is archaic usage. "Lazy" is the common lingo, but true sloth goes much deeper and has many levels. Sloth can be as deadly to a relationship as jealousy or pride. That is, if you get that far. A tub that has not been scrubbed since the Iran-Contra era can have you out the door before the nightcap is poured. Careful, though: Sloth can be much more subtle—like when you realize you're almost always the one to pick up the takeout, dry cleaning, or pets from the vet. And all this while your mate is, oh, I don't know, napping in preparation for watching TV later that night.

A while back, while pondering my own myriad levels of sloth as well as those displayed by the objects of my affections, my thoughts wandered to my girlfriend at the time, Isabelle. No, she is not lazy or slothful. She teaches tropical biology and knows quite a bit about sloths—the animal, that is—particularly the sloth that lives in the Amazon rain forest, which gets flooded yearly.

The sloth can live its entire life within a radius of two to three trees. The sloth moves so slowly that sometimes it will stay in the same trees for days because it takes too much effort to move. Compared with other mammals, the sloth actually has a reduced number of muscles. Once a week it comes down the tree to take care of its bodily functions. Need I say more?

In all fairness to the much maligned animal, I should add that when the Amazon floods, the sloth does swim and seem to enjoy it. Isabelle gave me a videotape, and if you could see how slowly these creatures move on land, it's amazing the species isn't extinct. One can't imagine any sloth having the energy to procreate. I'll bet it has a lot to do with proximity. "Well, he's only one branch over, and it does beat watching that dung beetle."

This creature is the perfect metaphor for some of the relationships I've been in. Sloth sets in after about a year.

Friday night rolls around, and trying to get your beloved off the couch is a task Sisyphus would shy away from—and this is the guy who's rolling that huge boulder up the hill, over and over again. She complains, "Let's stay in and watch pay-per-view—it's *Lethal Weapon 13*." Or, "There's weather out there and strangers—it's too hard."

In one long-term relationship I was in, a ridiculously long time had passed before I realized I was the one to carry all the groceries every time we shopped. At the checkout counter she'd say, "Oh, honey, I've got the car keys. Can you get that?" And unwittingly, I'd grab the two to three bags of groceries like a willing but not overly clever packhorse. One night two full years into the relationship, I caught on and was furious. She laughed long and hard. "I was wondering when you'd catch on," she chuckled. That's an example of a clever sloth.

That, by the way, is one of the attributes of the truly slothful: cleverly manipulating others to do the work while they basically watch the dung beetle. It can come right down to such seemingly small things as her always deferring to you to make the decisions. "No, you pick the restaurant, club, movie... I don't care." That way, they don't have to tax the delicate molecules in their brains with excessive thought. And, of course, the big plus: If it's a boring movie or bad meal, who takes the fall? Not her—that could create stress which takes energy, and a sloth has to save that energy for devising new strategies for getting out of cleaning.

So if you wake up and discover that your beloved is consistently taking a bath whenever the garbage needs to go out, or you've been flattered one time too many into running to the video store since you "always pick out the best films anyway," you're in love with a sloth. You have two choices: Resign yourself to doing all the work or make like the Amazon and threaten divorce—if the water gets high enough, they'll either sink or swim.

Vanity

This is one of the most common and embarrassing of the seven deadly sins. No, not the dressing table seen in all those black-and-white Joan Crawford movies. No, no, no—I mean the kind of heightened self-perception of one's supposedly good looks, achievements, or sexual prowess (to name but a few). Today, we call it ego, as in: "She has such an enormous ego she can only dine at places with double doors. Otherwise how *would* she get her head in?"

How do people get this way and how do we end up dating them—even once? How could we actually fall in love with them?

Vanity manifests in lots of personality types: There's the alternative kind of girl who says and does all the politically aware-isms. Most likely, they wear only cotton and are virulently vegetarian or vegan. (How can you eat something that has a face? Answer: Because it tastes good.) These people are driven to prove they are the most sensitive, most compassionate people who ever took a noninvasive step in their lives. They have a heightened sense of how important it is to the entire world infrastructure that they live on tofu and beets. I don't mean to diss my vegetarian friends—and since I live in San Francisco, that would be half the people in town—just the "How could you be anything but me?" types.

Now, how did I end up on a date with the above? Well, first of all, because I'm a lesbian, I didn't know if it was a date or just coffee. But when she winced when I put half-and-half in my coffee (you do dairy?!) I knew this was not going to be a date. More a mistake accompanied by copious amounts of caffeine and a shallow but clear NO.

I actually had a six-month affair with a very attractive, rather vain woman. Most people thought her pretty, as did I, so I was surprised when she courted me so ardently (I was in a tremendous bad-hair phase).

She brought me exotic sprays of flowers. Bundled to the back of her motorcycle, I road with her around the most beautiful city on earth on clear starry nights, kissing long and deep as though ours were the first kisses ever. Within two weeks after the start of our hyperromantic dating, she told me she was falling in love with me. I was smitten (read: in a lust-induced delusional state). She also had a hard athlete's body, that cool motorcycle, and a job in the "trades." In the late '80s in lesbian culture, she was "all that." And this fact was not lost on her *at all*.

Her vanity was subtle at first. She'd mention "so-and-so" having a crush on her—isn't that interesting? Absolutely, honey, thank you for lowering my self-esteem so it falls somewhere between adolescent insecurity and neurotic self-loathing. Thank you—honestly, it will make me stronger.

I realized she was not the ultimate lesbian lover of my dreams when she pointedly said something to the effect that because she was so good-looking, I might as well get used to all the flirting/passes of which she was the (willing) recipient.

Soon after that statement came the comment about it not being her fault that the "way society perceives women, I'm going to get hit on a lot more than you..." It was at this point that I jumped ship. I didn't care if I was destined to exclusively date trolls from that point on.

Overweening ego of that magnitude was more than even this baby dyke could take. She went out of town on a job, and when she came back I was gone. She also had a nasty temper. What a surprise, huh? How dare I dump her. After all, I was not the sexy femme fatale she was. How *dare* I dump her—it simply wasn't possible.

Actually, it had something to do with choosing between a relationship and my self-respect. Sorry. I didn't hate her because she was beautiful; I hated her because she was a self-centered, mean-spirited pig. Now, you know I didn't make this one up.

There's so much more to say about vanity—and I haven't even consulted my gay boyfriend Jim about some of the wackos he's dated. I haven't even touched on the "Look at my car/house/designer clothes that are so much better than you" type of vanity. Or Freud's theory of ego, superego, and colossal ego. (OK, I made up that last one.)

One cannot write about queer dating and vanity without some mention of the gay male notion that you *are* as good as you look. Full stop. If you are or look like a Hugo Boss model, you do not even have to pass go; you are already there, and *there* is where every other gay male wants to be. Before I get some folks up in arms, let me qualify: Not all gay men on the planet think this way. Rather, it is a culturally specific and readily observable phenomenon—just my way of saying wake up and smell the double nonfat latte.

This phenomenon became clear to me when I came out in the mid '80s. The men were all about looks; the women were all about emotional depth, and if that didn't appeal to you, you could always join a women's rugby team.

The men were always impeccably dressed and coiffed and three steps ahead of everyone else fashion-wise. Lesbians on the other hand, especially back then, made a point to be at least three steps behind the latest fashion, and we won't even talk hair. Conversely, gay men seemed to be so clean, it was as though they'd taken a metal brush to their bodies to achieve that overly scrubbed fresh look.

Now, the downside: What about the guys who no matter how hard they scrubbed, would be average-looking? Are they doomed to be dateless (though not trickless) since the ideal was out of their reach? And really, wasn't it all too shallow? Sure it was. But it was celebrated in so obvious a way you almost had to admire it.

I had a friend in high school—let's call him Michael. By the time he was 16, he was an out bisexual. A brave thing to do back then in Philadelphia, David Bowie and Boy George notwithstanding. He was short, dark, and very handsome. He looked very European—full-featured with olive skin with heavy-lidded crystal-green eyes, full sensual lips, and a strong jaw and cheekbones. He was also very insecure and vain about his looks. Even though he looked a cross between scary and silly coming to high school in full leathers on his motorcycle, I still admired his determination to be himself.

A couple years out of high school, I was waiting tables on the Jersey shore when some guy exclaimed, "Maureen! Oh, my God—it's so good to see you!" Not being able to place this guy, I timidly replied, "Hi...?"

"Maureen, it's me—Michael, Michael Euro-Cool (not his real name)." I tried my best not to look stunned. This Michael was unrecognizable from the one he was in high school. It wasn't just the bleached-blond hair—he'd obviously gotten a nose job. And it was really...odd: those large eyes and lips with this tiny Waspy nose. It was so disconcerting that I tried to look directly into his eyes for the remainder of the conversation.

He had been so handsome; now he was stuck with this teensy nose on the wrong face for all gay eternity. How much had the gay male culture of beauty influenced this unfortunate choice? A culture that allows for exploration of every vain dream you've ever had (I could be a Ralph Lauren clone! Really, bleach out my hair, clip the nose...). I don't know, but if Michael had turned out straight, wouldn't it have been a bit less likely for him to have gotten that nose job? No way to prove this, but drop-dead gorgeous straight guys rarely mess with what's already working.

Poor Michael, vanity victim. He was, by the way, still striking, those clear green eyes, but now in a kind of Picasso way. Not the effect he was going for, I'm sure. All that said, who among us wouldn't with enough encouragement and money augment something we saw as our worst physical "flaw"? For me, it's my chubby knees. If I could have them magically removed (not the knees, just the fat chunk that has taken up permanent residence on the inside part), I'd do it. But it would have to be paid for, painless, and completely foolproof. Emphasis on the fool.

Pride

Pride is one of the tricky deadly sins since it has so many connotations. There's of course the one I'll be discussing, the "pride cometh before the fall" aspect; but there's also civic pride, gay pride, taking pride in one's work, etc. Webster's lists 13 definitions—the two most interesting being numbers 8 and 10 respectively: a mettle in a horse and a company or group of lions. I'm glad I cleared that up—hate to have you thinking I'm dissing a group of lions. I'm going for the basic, "1. a high or inordinate opinion of one's dignity, importance, merit, or superiority, whether cherished in the mind or as displayed in bearing, conduct, etc." That was Webster's "etc." not mine. So confident that we all know what he means, even Webster doesn't need to list every annoying variation. Though, of course, I might, as details are my life.

First I want to recognize that there are levels of pride. I call low-level pride the sort that falls between self-respect and making yourself look good. Example: You finally get a date with the object of your abject desire. You are more than 30 minutes late. While you're rehearsing your excuses in your head, all designed to make you look good and at the same time convey to your date your sincere (abject) apologies, it would never occur to you to go the easy way—the truth. The truth that your favorite black trendy trousers were not to be found at the dry cleaners. Therefore, it took you an hour and a half to assemble an outfit that would cover all the bases and at the same time appear casual. Granted, no one in their right mind would tell that entire story, but the detailed traffic jam yarn is awfully tired.

Then there's the easy-to-spot prideful gal or guy—the lounge lizard. They always have the aforementioned "inordinate opinion of one's importance, merit, etc," and it's definitely in their minds. When they offer you a drink, it's always like it's the greatest honor bestowed on you since you won that Noble Prize.

In lesbian bars the ones who offer drinks in that smarmy way are often faux butches (I wouldn't insult my butch kindred by association). Sometimes they're actually quite good looking, but when you notice that having a regular seat at said bar is the center of their universe, you've got to wonder where all that swagger came from.

With gay men it's more often a money thing. They'll behave pretty much the same way, but after they offer the drink they'll be sure to look at their Rolexes in a conspicuous manner. I think the lesbian lounge lizards would do this too if any of them had Rolexes and if any of the rest of us knew what they looked like.

And let's not forget the charming person you met at a party, who later became the date from hell. Pride can insinuate itself subtly; after the first date you have no idea where your lack of self-worth is coming from. You begin to catch on when she asks you little things, like whether you "ride."

"Bicycles, subways, what?" you wonder.

She laughs in an amused, somewhat British way, "I meant

horses. Don't worry. I don't ride nearly as much as I used to anyway." It'll only be later that you'll think of all kinds of great comebacks: "Well, then, I'll bet there's a lot of happy horses!" Or, "Worry? Me? Why would I worry about your horse habits? What with being an overeducated, underpaid plebe who still takes the subway, and keeping the wolves from the door and all, I'm a pretty busy woman. Oh, that and spending the rest of my time hoping that someday I'll date a woman who rides horses." I wonder if her horse has a mettle.

Proud people are often very exclusive about who they hang out with, which means most of us are safe. Unfortunately, we're not safe from our own twisted moments of "bad" pride. For instance, once a very attractive woman was clearly entranced by my red hair. She asked if it was real, and I replied with my inordinate sense of importance, "Not anymore." Please! I had what my mother referred to as "red highlights" until I was 10. Not anymore? Pride, the bad kind, always gags you if you have any moral compass at all. Unfortunately, mostly after the fact.

Greed

Greed takes many forms. For lesbians, if you're not especially butch/femme-identified, how do you work out who pays after the first date? I hate splitting the bill with any date. I'd rather pay or take turns. By the third date, if she hasn't offered to pick up the dinner check or buy the movie tickets, even once, it's over. O-V-E-R. That's unabashed greed. More money for her, less for you. And I begin to feel like a pathetic loser who has to pay to get a good-night kiss out of another woman. Plus, who doesn't like to be treated special? Showered with dinners, gifts, trips to Paris? OK, in my fantasies I'm greedy, but she's always enormously wealthy too.

My gay boyfriend, Jim, told me a story about a lawyer he dated briefly (no pun intended). Let's call him Roger. Roger was *all* that: gym-fit, smart, handsome, drove a Mercedes convertible. At the time, Jim was a bartender and was also gym-fit, smart, and handsome, but he rode the bus. Jim described to me how whenever the cocktail waiter would come toward them with their drinks, suddenly Roger would either go to the men's room or became heavily involved in checking his pockets, presumably for a wallet. Jim kept paying for the drinks. The first few times Jim didn't care; in fact, he wanted to pay because he didn't want their income difference to be an issue.

Their second date was a sleepover (amazing restraint on Jim's part). In the morning Jim was the one to run out for bagels, O.J., and coffee, since there wasn't a scrap of food in Roger's tastefully appointed flat. Roger thanked him with a kiss, but no offer to pay or even chip in. On date 3, the pattern held: more dashing to the men's room, more endless pocket searches for mysterious *missing things*. So Jim calmly asked the cocktail waiter to run a tab (while ol' Rog was in the men's room). He proceeded to drink numerous $10-a-pop snifters of top-shelf brandy. Then he asked to be excused to go to the men's room, never to be seen again. I almost stood up and applauded Jim. What goes around comes around, and gay men do revenge better than anyone else. Except maybe exceptionally high-femme straight women who know how to dispatch a cheap creep in style themselves.

There are worse cases of greed—particularly in divorces with joint property holdings, stock portfolios, etc. But since I have no experience with those things myself, I hesitate to comment. Besides, it's mostly not funny—at all. I had a friend of a friend who was going through a breakup so acrimonious that when one woman moved out she actually forced the one who stayed to divide *everything* in the kitchen equally. Including bringing over her own empty jars to split up the spices. They even, bag by bag, divided all the boxes of herbal tea (and with lesbians that could be 50 boxes or more). This might fall into the petty/cheap category, but the underlying emotion is greed. I want what you have and then some. And I'm sure the one equipped with jars snuck in more than her fair share of tea bags.

The one good thing about being an overeducated, poor artist is you can always give a loved one half of what you have. At the end of most months in my life, that will buy you an exquisite single red rose. And that's not a bad thing.

Lust and Deceit

In the area of relationships gone wrong, these two go together like salt and pepper, yin and yang, coconuts and large breasted women. (OK, maybe not that last one, unless you live in Hawaii and have some campy girlfriends with a penchant for wearing fruit as undergarments.)

Lust in and of itself is a good thing. It is our reward for staying alive. When one is in a monogamous relationship, it is particularly helpful to lust after your monog-babe. Should you be having fits of unbridled lust for others and act on them, that's where deceit comes in—in droves. It's called cheating. Therefore, LUST + DECEIT = CHEATING. Two cardinal sins for the price of one.

It seems to me that the term *cheating* is an odd word choice for something that potentially can ruin your life. Let me explain: I cheat on my income "level" to credit card companies; everyone cheats on their driver's license weight (I myself get a bit taller). These are not things that are going to impact one's life in a dramatic and tragic way. However, if your *life partner* turns out to be *cheating* on you, that can lower your self-esteem from 900 to zero in less time than it takes to tie your shoes. And it's going to hurt. Bad.

Of course, cheating is a lot more complicated than that, especially given various sexual orientations. I took a survey of my gay-girl friends' opinions of those women who leave their LTR (long-term relationship) for a lover, or in '50s speak, the "other woman." The consensus: The "other woman" is usually just a springboard for getting out of a relationship that the wayward partner was otherwise too chickenshit to end. This springboard effect does not bode well for the "new" relationship. In fact, I've only known one couple who started this way whose relationship lasted longer than a year. It's the old "If she did it to her, she'll do it to you" syndrome.

Me, I've never been big on cheating, since it always seems much simpler to break up a relationship with a current lover before indulging with another. Granted, none of these instances involved long-term lovers, so maybe I just got lucky. I'm also the world's worst liar. And being relatively scatter-brained and a talker, the odds of my keeping my story straight are up there with Donald Trump turning his empire into a model socialist commune.

This is not to say I haven't been tempted. Once, while in a LTR, I was hit on by a woman so sexy and beautiful I could barely breathe. She gave me one of those smoldering, direct across-the-room looks. My first response was to look behind me, wondering *whom* she was staring at. To think, all that hot sizzling energy directed solely at me was unheard-of, especially when I already had a GF. To make things worse, at the time my girlfriend and I were in a very rocky period (and actually broke up three months later).

My first reaction was to run away—literally. The woman approached me and without any reason, tact, or semblance of grace, I ran away. Truly—I picked up my coat and fled. So intimidated was I to feel so attracted to a woman who was not my partner. Later, though, I thought about her all the time—I mean, all the time. Unbidden in the middle of work or a lecture at school, there she'd be, obscuring everything else—sounds, sight, control of one's saliva. She was my secret "thought candy."

I knew I wouldn't act on it, but in my imagination I did. Is that cheating, or merely healthy cathartic daydreaming during a stressful period? The other reason I don't believe in cheating: It's just not respectful to your lover or yourself. But so many of us do it. Wonderful people, I know, have done it. It just…happens.

Large or small, gay-girl communities more than frown on cheating. Think: "You'll never date in this town again."

I have a close friend who, ever since her LTR of six years

ended eight years ago, has consistently fallen in love with married, separated, or "not sure where their relationship is at women"—as if you could lose a relationship like a wallet.

My friend is gorgeous, smart, well-employed, witty, and spiritual. Not one of these women, despite promises and assurances that they would leave their LTR for her, has ever done so. One clandestine relationship lasted more than three years. I watched my friend go through emotional hell, seek professional help, join 12-step programs, go to ashrams, consult crystals—you name it. Still she goes for the unattainable.

Even she admits there must be some part of her that gets something out of this. Is it the escape hatch of the married? The adrenaline rush of the hidden, dark secret that only the two of you share? Is it the basic challenge of having what isn't yours? Will any of us ever know?

Then there's the "emotional" affair. That's when you do everything but sex. Some people consider this just as deadly. You're cut off from your partner, who consistently prefers someone else's company, while you watch them carry on from the sidelines. Since they are not "doing it" or even kissing, there's not a lot you can do. You could forbid your partner to see that person again, but of course that would probably throw them into each other's waiting arms. No, I say make lots of plans with your own friends. Then, when you can fit it in, ask your absentee girlfriend on a hot date and seduce the hell out of her.

What does this all mean? One thing I know for sure: Cheating stinks. For many gay girls, it's an unfortunate aspect of serial monogamy. These are gross generalizations, of course; the more important point is that cheating always ends up hurting someone. Above all, it is wise to remember that cliché: What goes around, comes around.

There you have it: seven major reasons you can wake up next to someone who is not your dream girl and most definitely should not make the short list for "life partners." People can change, but on the big things, that change is *slow*. Usually, you don't win by staying with the person. Somehow once a dynamic is in place with two people, there's no way for one to go through massive self-growth without the other one getting so much fallout. The phrase "buried alive" comes to mind. But hey, that's just me.

Epilogue: The Romantic Versus the Cynic

What is there to say? I remain an optimistic romantic, no matter how much evidence to the contrary I accrue. How do I do this? I give myself short periods of intense hands-off "don't even look my way" cynicism.

It's all about balance. Not your yoga/meditation "at one with the earth" type of balance (that's for those more evolved than me). It's more a somewhat twisted but ultimately healthy attitude about romance, sex, love, and all the itchy things in between.

I know that some affairs will grow and shock me at a depth of feeling I can in fact have; some, more pheromonally induced, will burn fast and hot, while others will be mellow and sweet. On occasion, I get burned so badly that I leap unbidden into the vat of grief that is always lying in wait for me, like a greedy San Francisco landlord waiting for a tenant to move out so he or she can triple the rent. After I wallow in the vat a while, I resurface in varying stages of anger, then go through a lovely calm followed by a gradual return to self-respect.

That's where cynicism comes in handy. It repels women like an overflowing sewer. Who wants to hit on a someone who thinks all dating and romance is a waste of time and only lands you back in the same place—only by now, while you were too busy rearranging your personality and self-worth, the world has moved on. In fact, it's ahead of you by at least 30-plus miles. Oh, and you have no car, bike, or skateboard, and the bus only comes when it feels like it.

All you can do is stand there and wait and watch the world recede into the distance, getting smaller and smaller as it trudges on. One day, when say you actually manage to sleep through the night, you realize that either (1) you might as well start walking, or (2) the bus is in fact coming, but you don't have the right change. The trick in the latter situation is to get on the bus anyway and ask if anyone can break a $20 bill. It's at this point that some stranger, seeing your slept-in clothes and general disarray, will take pity on you and pay your fare. Your belief in the essential goodness of people will return as you gratefully grab a window seat.

In the former case—it's a long walk. It will be either too hot or too cold, depending on which you hate more. The good thing is that along the way you'll see other people waiting for the bus. Some will join you; others won't. You won't like those who join you that much, because they're all sort of crabby from waiting so long too for the damn bus.

Fortunately, exhaustion is the great equalizer. By the time you catch up with the world, you'll have respect for people's fortitude and determination, even if they were a touchy, disgruntled bunch to begin with. Remember, so were you. This will lead to respect for their strength, which will lead you back to your own self-respect and before you know it, you've had a shower, a hot meal, and are surrounded by the world again.

Ah, romance, that endorphin rush that is more potent

than mainlining heroin or running a marathon. But it's not only that. It's that there's a person who loves you, even though you always transpose numbers and end up at the wrong address nine times out of 10. There's a person who loves you, even if you don't know or care what a postmodern metaphor is. She understands why you cry during an especially close basketball game (not that you're playing—you're just watching the game on TV). It's the all in the details.

I hate the expression that you'll find someone when you stop looking. Not true. Too many people I know who are out there meeting people and doing things end up with more dates/romances. I think what might be more accurate is that being needy is unattractive and will send prospective dates running to the nearest bus shelter. That falls under of category of looking with a vengeance, and that is not a good idea.

Another romantic ideal: the idea of meeting your other *half.* That one nauseates me. We weren't *halves* as children, so why should romantic love create this unmeshed "Where do I end and where do you begin?" myth of perfect romantic love? I visualize it like something out of *The X Files* (when David Duchovny was still on the show): Your body and soul ooze into the cracks and crevices of the other person and vice versa. A lot of dripping goo Scully can't identify keeps reappearing. It's not pretty. Fittingly, it's another unsolved X File.

There's no trick to it. It's the most basic of basics: Love yourself and your life and there will be plenty of love and life in your life. I know that sounds redundant (and also very hard, which it can be), but think about it. The future is now. Don't wait until you have that perfect gay girl on your arm. Begin without her. You never know—she might stop by.

Acknowledgments

Love is a many-splendored thing, especially if you have a bunch of riotous girlfriends of the nonlover variety. I am eternally indebted to my pals who listened to or read my first drafts and inspired some of these essays, and whose keen eye reined me in—especially Chris Peloquin, Rhonda Coffman, and Lynnly Labovitz. Thanks also to my terrific editor, Angela Brown, whose many great suggestions make me look ever so much more coherent, and without whom this book never would have existed. To my friend, author Phyllis Burke, who while inscribing her latest book to me, told me it wouldn't be long before I'd be inscribing my book to her. I had no idea what she was talking about.

To my many friends who either contributed their love-life stories, and/or gave emotional, moral, caffeine, or sugar support: Veronique LaCapra, Pamela August Russell, Karla Carmony, Trish McDermott, Karen Dzienkowski, Tracey Rose, Nan O'Connor, Jody Cole, Neen Nicholson, "Sheila," Jaylek, Blanca Coma, Petra Griffith, Joe Heavey, Heather Cassell, Jack Collins, Allison King, Susan Oekler, and Jim Minteer. Obviously, to all my exes, past dates, or infatuations: If you think you've found yourself in these pages, remember it's fiction—really. To my big sis Donne and her daughter Meredith, who six years ago at the tender age of 7 told her mother that she really loved Xena—in fact, so much so that she exclaimed, and I quote, "Mama, I might be the kind of girl who's built for a woman!" When I asked my sister how she felt about this, she said, "Are you kidding? Boys? High school? I'd be thrilled!" Clearly, I've had my sister's support every gay-girl step of the way. And some of those steps were over cliffs. Also to my brother-in-law, Peter, who for years now in his best back-woods accent has teased me with, "You got yourself some of them woman problems again, Mo?" They say you don't get to choose your family, but sometimes you get lucky. I did.